# Jeremy Beecham

## A Quiet Altruist

Jon Gower Davies

Editor

ERGO PRESS
HEXHAM

# JEREMY BEECHAM
## A QUIET ALTRUIST

ISBN: 978-0-9934330-1-6

Cover Graphics: Mark Rogerson
mark@jollycreative.org
Typeset: Alan I Grint
alan.grint@yahoo.com

Print North East Limited
NE6 1LH

Our thanks to NCJ Media
for permission to use the image of
Clara Street, Benwell, in 1960

ERGO PRESS
HEXHAM
writeonediting@yahoo.com

# CONTENTS

*Prologue:* Richard and Sara Beecham

*Introduction:* Jon Gower Davies

*In the beginning ... early socialism and good friends*

*Benwell and the Toon*

## London calling

## Transcribed Interviews, 2020 and 1995

*"Over an extraordinary 55 years spent in public service, Jeremy touched and transformed the lives of so many, from community to region to country. A skilful and driven politician and warm and witty man, he has inspired admiration and respect both within the Labour family and across the political divide. Jeremy's legacy is exceptional and that is rightly celebrated in this book."*

Sir Tony Blair

## *Prologue*

### Richard and Sara Beecham

When Jon Davies initially approached us with the idea of compiling a book of thought-pieces, recollections and reminiscences about Dad to mark his retirement as a Newcastle City Councillor after fifty-five years of unbroken service, we were uncertain. Dad has never been one to blow his own trumpet, always preferring to get on with the job quietly in the background rather than grandstanding in public. However, we have been won over by the warmth and affection the book's contributors so evidently feel towards Dad as both a colleague and friend, as well as the high regard in which they hold him as a politician, even if they don't all share his political views. Now that Dad has retired from both the House of Lords and City Council and stepped back from over half-a-century of public life, we feel that he can afford to bask in some praise and recognition (enlivened with a bit of judicious criticism!) although he will doubtless respond to the book with a customary raised eyebrow and wittily self-deprecating quip (but also, perhaps, with a little inward glow).

Despite our close relationship with Dad, we have known little of the detail of his working life, both locally and nationally, over the years. So this book has made for an interesting and illuminating read. Of course, we grew up in a household where Dad's love (bordering on obsession) for Newcastle, for Benwell and for the Labour Party was in the very air we

Left to right, Richard, Sara and Jeremy with tennis legend Bjorn Borg
during the *Newcastle 900* celebrations.

breathed. We have many happy childhood memories related to Newcastle politics: Dad driving us around Benwell on local election days whilst we handed out Labour stickers through the car windows to local kids and took turns on the tannoy to broadcast "Vote Labour, vote Beecham, vote now!" in our high-pitched voices; the excitement of helping out (or more likely hindering) on election days at Yvonne Bell's Labour HQ in Fenham (Yvonne was Dad's stalwart Civic Centre secretary) during which we would deliver leaflets, knock on doors to get the vote out and number-take at the scout-hut polling station; rampaging up and down the marble corridors and grand staircase of the Civic Centre on visits to see Dad at work during school holidays. And we met a host of VIPs at civic events – the 1970s tennis super-star, Bjorn Borg, was a highlight for us, the Labour Prime Minister, Jim Callaghan, rather less so – whilst Sara was given the honour (or, for her, the stress) of presenting a bouquet of flowers to the Queen Mother at the *Newcastle 900* celebrations. Happy memories. Happy days.

Although not all of our memories are quite so happy: there was the time in the late 1970s when the National Front daubed their insignia on the exterior wall of our family home in Gosforth and, in another anti-Semitic attack, a pig's trotter was thrown through the door of our neighbours' house, mistaking it for ours. And in between the many good folk from Benwell who would phone Dad to speak with their councillor about a ward matter, there were the not infrequent callers who ranted abuse down the phone at whichever one of us was unlucky enough to have picked up the receiver first.

But for every abusive caller there were a hundred smiling strangers who would approach Dad, unprompted, on the street with that fond and familiar Geordie greeting: "Y'alreet Jeremy?" In his quiet, modest, un-showy way, he was a bit of a local celebrity, our Dad. And we remain as proud of him today as we were then, a man passionate about social justice and utterly devoted to serving the city he loves.

Sara presenting the Queen Mother with a bouquet
during the *Newcastle 900* celebrations.

# Introduction

Jon Gower Davies

This book, or anthology, is part history, part biography: Newcastle upon Tyne appears as history, and Jeremy Beecham, or Lord Beecham as he now is, is the subject of the biography. Nearly all of the contributors are familiar with – that is not just knowledgeable about – both of these, the history and the biography. I, for example, have lived and worked in Newcastle for nearly all of my married and working life. I spent twenty years on Newcastle City Council with Jeremy, not always agreeing with him, but admiring his political skills. A few weeks ago, at his home in Gosforth, and after yet another defeat at Scrabble, I once again experienced the adeptness of his way with words. Whereas I was deselected by my Labour comrades, Jeremy went through 55 years on the council, as well as serving on the AGA and later in the House of Lords. Contributors such as Tony Flynn, Peter Morris, David Goldwater, Lord Shipley, and Jonathan Blackie are – like me – friends and ex-colleagues of Jeremy: we live nearby and our lives are, in one way or another, caught up in his.

In a way, biographies are the easier of the two to grasp. The history of a city is much more contentious. Cities embroider, advertise and camouflage their histories through, for example, monuments, street names and identified buildings. In this way, amongst other ways, the identities, contributions (and aggrandisements) of individual people are broadcast to the millions of pedestrians who walk through and busy themselves in the brick and stone stories of the city in which they live. Newcastle upon Tyne is one such city – the name itself is a clue, though not many will know the actual date of the building of the 'new' castle (1080AD), or that it was plonked on top of a much older Roman fortress. In 1980, biography and history interacted, when Jeremy – against my wishes – set in motion a celebration of 900 years since the arrival of the Normans: he did not agree with me that they were a bunch of bullies. As was often the case he had his way, and the Queen Mother came to help him celebrate the onset of Norman dominance. At the moment, there seems to be little public recognition of the Roman bridge, *Pons Aelius*, built by Hadrian 1900 years ago, which crossed the Tyne, connecting the fort at Chester-le-Street with the Roman Wall which was later extended to *Segedunum*.

More modern history is expressed in various urban structures, statues and monuments, which celebrate, in masonry, the identities and achievements of the most influential men (usually men) of the city – Earl Grey, George Stephenson, Lord Armstrong and other great scientists and benefactors, sportsmen and business men, architects and developers. Amongst these men deserving of monument are politicians: Earl Grey was MP for Northumberland, as well as Prime Minister, while the coalminer Thomas Burt was the first working class man to hold ministerial office in London. In 1932 the monument to Earl Grey was rededicated: "in gratitude", it states, "to Earl Grey, for a century of civil peace". By this, as I understand it, the local leaders of those days regarded the gradual broadening of the franchise as the means whereby this country avoided the civil wars which so afflicted many other Western countries. Jeremy's life is, I think, proof of the validity of this variant of our national history. Jeremy Beecham worked in the world created by the electoral franchise proclaimed on Grey's Monument. He was Leader of the City Council from 1977 to 1994, retiring in 2022 after 55 years of service at a local level. Over those years, in an extraordinary way, he amalgamated local with national politics in living proof of what it states on the back of our monument.

At this time there were many changes going on in the city, and many of these derived from Jeremy's initiatives. Yet there is nothing in the city which asks you to recognise him apart from a modest cul-de-sac in his electoral ward, a room in a local library and a wooden bench dedicated to his lovely wife, Brenda, in a small public space just off the A1. Compare this with the monument to Earl Grey. A recent exhibition on the contribution of local Jews to the North East and Newcastle made no mention of Lord Jeremy Beecham. Other prominent Jewish politicians, such as Charlie Slater of Sunderland, are also not mentioned.

Yet Jewishness – whatever one means by that – was not always so invisible. On occasion, in the early days of his political presence, Jeremy sought Labour nomination for Parliament. While he did once get a nomination for Tynemouth, where he lost to Irene Ward, he was never nominated for a seat in Newcastle itself, and that was – as I witnessed directly – in part because of the anti-Semitism which then (and now?) lurks within some parts of the Labour Party: I knew Labour Party members, friends of mine, who as left-wing politicians and as committed Christians, would not support his nomination because he was a Jew. I could not, and cannot, understand this. Prejudice finds some strange homes.

This 'blockage' does not of course explain why he was so obviously absent from the recent exhibition about the role of Jews in the North East, made all the more odd because Jeremy is alive and living in the city which owes so much to him. To an extent, this casual oblivion is perhaps due to his own remarkable self-effacing reticence: he neither seeks nor wants personal recognition. Perhaps this also explains why so often in the many books which have been written about Newcastle and Tyneside (including my own) he's barely visible. In between games of Scrabble and chats with Jeremy, I wander around charity shops buying books from the 'Local Interest' section. What we tend to find in these books is a recurring promotion of a much earlier, and very different local politician: T. Dan Smith. This odd genealogy is not just personal, but reflects two eras of political and architectural history. Once upon a time, in the world of town and country planning, some variant of 'new town' was seen as the best alternative to the decaying bombed rubble of our Victorian slum-cities: certainly, in Newcastle under T. Dan Smith, planning was accorded an activist vigour which for a while dominated our space. Newcastle has its own share of inheritance from those days – concrete, glass, and motorcars free to roam. *New* equalled *good*. There were those who felt that Newcastle had become the 'empire on which the concrete never set'.

In Jeremy's time, but not necessarily because of him, 'new' took a back seat: thus, for example, little more than 30% was ever built of the concrete motorways planned to criss-cross the city. Little mention is made in the accounts of those days of Jeremy's attitudes to such changes. Thus, for example, in a book I recently found in Oxfam, T. Dan Smith gets *five* references, Jeremy gets *one* (and I get *one*, too). In this book we find a favourable reference to TDS – "flawed but ambitious" – and then we read:

> Since his [TDS's] departure (on account of involvement in corruption) ... there is serious absence of leadership and vision in Tyneside, and there are no local leaders with access to national centres of power.[1]

Once again, Jeremy has disappeared. Yet as we shall see, his consistent good sense did indeed give him access to 'national centres of power', and – in spite of the nonsense just quoted – the good folk now writing this anthology know how much the city owes to him. At least four of us served for years on the City Council, some at the same time as Jeremy, some after him. Some of us worked with him as employees of the council. Others worked alongside him through, for example, voluntary organisations or with central government-inspired schemes such as the Urban Development Corporation under which major more or less beneficial changes took place in the heart of our city. Apart from the Local Government Association, he oversaw a review of local public services in – of all places – Wales, sat on the Historic Buildings and Monuments Committee for England, and was endlessly busy in a variety of national bodies of both political and

1. Robinson F, *Post-Industrial Tyneside*, Newcastle City Libraries, 1988, p. 216

practical natures. Some of our local schemes, such as for example the very great and very important Interceptor Sewer, predated Jeremy and other local politicians and administrators who contribute to this book, and like us, Jeremy was to some extent quite unaware of certain things. His and our minds were focussed on more immediate matters. However – and it is a big however – anyone using a bus pass should nod a head in thanks to the man who got it carried through central government. More details of his strengths and diffidences (or indifferences) follow.

In initiating this book, I remember the twenty years I served with Jeremy on the City Council. When, these days, I go and play Scrabble with him (he wins, he cheats) inevitably we engage in reminiscence. While my political career was only local and came to an abrupt and comradely end, as I said, Jeremy played a very active role in the Local Government Association and later in the House of Lords. He wrote, and had published, hundreds of letters to The Guardian. It is only very recently that he quit the council and now lives, well looked after, about half a mile from me, and indeed close to several other contributors to this book. It should be stressed again, I think, that while he served so well and so long at a local level, he also took his skills and style into the national system of government and administration. No one more than he demolishes the fallacies underlying the current obsession with 'levelling up': no one, no system, can rival Jeremy Beecham as both proponent, precursor and example of 'levelling up'.

For much of the time we write about, he was the leader of the local Labour Party and of the City Council. Most of the time – though not all – he and I got on, motivated above all by a desire to act in the interests of the city, harassed as it too often by rival neighbouring local authorities (Labour controlled!) and by the London-addicted antics of central government. No country in Europe is now so devoid of genuine local government as we are: we live in the most unitary state in Europe. For a while under Jeremy's leadership, the City Council had a degree of independent revenue, when we were free of the condescensions of London-derived 'plans' for our 'deprived' areas. The City Council owned over half of the city's land area, and half of all houses. As we shall see, the weight of this ownership was not, under Jeremy's leadership, slewed or bridled by leftist ambitions such as affected parts of London and Liverpool at the time. The main problem, in the years of his leadership, was to restrain not left-wing excoriations or capitalist greed, but the inheritance of the T. Dan Smith era, which if pursued would have seen an avalanche of concrete obliterating the city's past. Together we ensured, I trust, that Newcastle will avoid becoming nothing but a 'new town', with its history eradicated by bulldozers and cement mixers. In a way, we have all been conservative – though not all the folk writing here will agree. We write, and you read.

And as you read, have in mind this: the technical skills needed for the production of this book came from Alan and Julia Grint of Hexham. Freely and cheerfully they dealt with all matters to do with the publication. I am indeed very grateful to them. Without them, no book.

Read on!

*In the beginning …*
*early socialism and good friends*

"Some of us would walk to the Bigg Market, Newcastle's version of Speaker's Corner, where a soapbox was all you needed to gather a crowd and start a lively debate ... it's where Jeremy honed his skills."

Fiona Clarke

*Jeremy kept the whole carriage entertained with his quips …*

Jeremy's fame preceded him: my father, the local Labour Party Chairman, had already been impressed by his precocious talent and eloquence, seeing him as a great prospect for the future, when I met him for the first time at the Labour Committee Rooms. This was at a by-election in the Arthur's Hill ward of Newcastle when I was around 12 or 13 and Jeremy about 15. I don't remember much about that encounter, except his confidence, ebullience and sense of humour. He wasn't a physically imposing young man, but he drew people to him with his warmth. He was very mature for his age.

Over the next few years we met weekly at the Sunday evening sessions of the Newcastle North Young Socialists held at 5 Winchester Terrace, a stately slum property just off the West Road, which was the headquarters of the constituency party. We convened in a large, ground floor room, and made less than hygienic tea in a damp, dark kitchen in the basement. Jeremy was the chair of our teenage activists, and I was the secretary … albeit a very bad one, who seldom kept the minutes properly.

We sometimes arranged speakers from the local party, or visiting politicians from outside the area, including a few big names like Anthony Crosland MP, and afterwards some of us would walk to the Bigg Market, Newcastle's version of Speaker's Corner, where a soapbox was all you needed to gather a crowd and start a lively debate. I remember a fine Communist speaker, and a number of odd religious sectarians keen to save our souls. We were mainly there to heckle; it's where Jeremy honed his skills.

Our YS branch would have looked very strange to the workers of Tyneside. We were mostly recruited from two highly selective, direct grant schools: the Royal Grammar School, where Jeremy had a loyal following, and Central High School across the road, where there was a group of like-minded 'bolshie' girls. 'Left-wing intellectuals' would have been one way of describing us, but we were also part of a wider local youth movement, *The 59 Society*, started a year or two earlier and affiliated to the Labour Party. Most of its founding members were a couple of years older than us, but similarly intellectual, and mainly on the left wing of the party. The long-suffering Regional Youth Organiser, Ron Evers, tried to keep us in order. He arranged gatherings, notably at Otterburn Hall, a tea-total venue where the older lads used to smuggle in alcohol. Jeremy wasn't one of them.

There was turmoil in those days of the early 60s, with a plethora of left-wing splinter parties and groups, both outside and within the Labour Party. This was also the time of CND and the Aldermaston Marches against Britain's possession of nuclear weapons. I don't know how Jeremy developed his political ideas, but they were well-formed at an early age; he was quick to distance himself from any form of capitalism, which earned him respect among his peers. He was always a centrist, moderate member of the Labour Party – often in friendly conflict with those of us who were more rebellious left-wingers – but he always enjoyed the debate, and was a good friend.

Jeremy must have departed for university before me, and later gained his legal qualifications while I was away from Newcastle. His future wife, Brenda Woolf, was another associate of the Young Socialists, and moved in the same group of friends, although I never thought of her as a political animal. It was no surprise to the rest of us that the two became engaged and married. Brenda seemed the perfect partner: vivacious, engaging and down to earth. In their many years together she was a stabilising force for Jeremy when he was sometimes overwhelmed by the pressures of leadership. It may well have been his desire to be with Brenda and his family that confirmed his decision to remain local and influence policy from his home base in Newcastle rather than to pursue a seat in Parliament.

As a councillor for Benwell, Jeremy was well-liked and readily available for constituents, despite his growing influence both locally and nationally. I left Newcastle in 1965 and didn't move back until 1977 with my young family. My return brought me closer to Brenda Beecham: both of us were active in the National Childbirth Trust. Brenda had her own interests, well away from politics; I suspect that this was a deliberate strategy to maintain her identity and to keep busy while Jeremy was absorbed by politics.

Jeremy didn't often join Brenda in her activities, though I do remember a dinner with the famous French obstetrician Frederick Leboyer (author of *Birth Without Violence*), where in spite of being in unfamiliar waters Jeremy showed his usual flair for entertaining conversation. Brenda also travelled widely in pursuit of her passion for circle dancing, making friends across the world. She bore her later illness with typical fortitude and made a positive contribution to research and publicity about bowel cancer.

I once shared a railway carriage with Jeremy, sitting towards the rear, when the train was brought to a lengthy halt. While we were waiting for information about the cause of the delay, Jeremy kept the whole carriage entertained with his quips. This was typical of his wit and quick thinking, which I'm sure was one of the ways he gained support for his political position. I can imagine his role in the House of Lords, forensically analysing legislation from the perspective of his enduring passion for equity and support for those in need.

Jeremy is also a passionate supporter of Newcastle United and has been a season-ticket holder for many years. After suffering the Mike Ashley era, the Saudi-led take-over must be an even greater trial for him …

Among his many strengths Jeremy is a loyal friend, and all those who know him will surely wish him well now that he has stepped back from public life.

Fiona Clarke

*Jeremy would rush off to get the best lox and bagels for breakfast.*

A fourteen year old naïve, enthusiastic and over-idealistic Young Socialist, I first met Jeremy in the early 1960s at meetings in the Labour Party office on Winchester Terrace in Elswick. He cajoled and charmed us away from arguing – and socialising – to the footslog of delivering leaflets in the ward that he would represent for over fifty years. His many other distinguished public service achievements are well documented, and I followed these as an observer once I had moved from Newcastle. Despite these accolades, to me he has always been just a great friend who gave a speech at my wedding, and who is as loyal to his friends as he is to his electors.

Jeremy's marriage and family life were rooted in the profound love and respect he and Brenda found for each other as teenagers. They were as intensely loving when I saw them together for the last time, shortly before Brenda died in 2010, as on their wedding day in 1968. Brenda was warm, feisty, clever and full of humour; she gave Jeremy a levity he might otherwise have lacked. Together they created a secure home for their children, Sara and Richard, from where they all pursued their varied interests – a home that was open and welcoming to people like me. That all sounds far too complacent: theirs was a place to argue about politics and culture, to share experiences and family news, to enjoy banter, wit and laughter.  And to eat. Food was important and Jeremy would rush off to get the best lox and bagels for breakfast. His other great love is, of course, Newcastle and its people. He is proud to belong there.

Our lives touch regularly with Christmas cards, oddly marking a belief that neither of us hold. Key memories are of scurrying after him from the Civic Centre to St James Park to watch a match: Jeremy walks faster than anyone I know! Of watching him introduce Tony Blair at a Nottingham rally when "things could only get better", and for a while they did. Of his 60th birthday party, complete with a Geordie ranter. Of the gift of the book *Fire and Fury* about Donald Trump for my 70th birthday.

Jeremy managed to retain his moral compass and integrity to rise above the hurt and damage he felt acutely in the wake of political betrayals, corruption and disloyalty … to go on doggedly using his political nous and skills to better the lives of people who needed it most, when he could have backed off into his law practice. With dignity he dealt with the ugly antisemitism he experienced, and with the misery of the Labour Party's inability or unwillingness to act against it, even so recently.

Jeremy values his friends, and I am one among others from those Young Socialist days with whom he has linked up from time to time for meals together and of whom we talk fondly. Such lifelong friendships are rare. His enriches my life.

Heather Roberts

*"That's a good idea!" Thank you, Jeremy.*

Many of the recent tributes to Jeremy on his retirement have, quite rightly and understandably, focussed on his outstanding record in local government and his great contribution in that role at local, regional and national levels.

However, I would like to talk about two other aspects of his work and life. First, about Jeremy's political career outside local government, particularly in the House of Lords, and secondly, on Jeremy's career and work as a solicitor – given that he was my family's solicitor for over forty years.

I first met Jeremy when he was chosen in the 1960s to be our Labour candidate in Tynemouth, standing against Dame Irene Ward. I remember my mother enthusing about our new, young candidate, and how pleased she was that he'd been selected. I was amazed to discover that we were both the same age, as he seemed so calm, wise and committed! We were all convinced that he would make an excellent MP, and were very disappointed when he failed to be elected in 1970, where Labour lost power and Harold Wilson was voted (temporarily) out of office.

Before that, in 1968, when my father sadly died, we needed a solicitor, and Jeremy was the obvious choice. Again, I remember how calm, efficient and helpful he was at that sad time. Ever afterwards he remained our first choice whenever we needed a solicitor or legal advice. We even joke that, much later, Jeremy was responsible for my marriage to Guy, because when we asked him to act for us in buying a house together he explained the legal advantages of being married when doing so. We looked at each other and thought, "That's a good idea!" Thank you, Jeremy.

Baron Beecham of Benwell and Newcastle upon Tyne

Jeremy's later career in the House of Lords was another huge success, given his contribution to Labour both in local government and on Labour's National Executive Committee. It was no surprise that he was very rapidly appointed to Labour's front bench as a shadow minister. He became one of Labour's key spokespeople, and commanded great respect across the House of Lords for his grasp of the issues and for the measured yet compelling arguments he deployed, enhanced by his gentle, effective sense of humour. This approach was perfect for the non-confrontational atmosphere that normally prevails in the House of Lords. Yet you could never be in any doubt about the sincerity and deep political conviction that always informed Jeremy's words whenever he stood up at the dispatch box.

I was lucky enough to share an office, *The Geordie Cell*, with Jeremy from the time he entered the House of Lords until his retirement, and during this time we became even better friends. It was wonderful sharing an office with someone in whom you had absolute trust and confidence. We also had a good many laughs, and gave each other mutual support when politics turned sour and crazy, with Labour election defeats, the Brexit referendum and the election of Boris Johnson as Prime Minister. Jeremy never wavered in his belief that a better future could be achieved and that Labour – and his beloved North East – would flourish and prosper together in that brighter future for the UK as a whole.

While many people know Jeremy's family better that I do, I have happy memories of Brenda – including her attempts as a style guru to give me advice and help on colours, outfits and making a favourable visual impression! I have also been very struck by Sara and Richard's love for their parents; by their constant support and appreciation of Jeremy. Meeting up with Richard on a couple of occasions in recent months has been a great pleasure for me, and I know how quietly and steadfastly proud Jeremy rightly is of both him and of Sara.

In his many roles, Jeremy's achievements have been countless, but in retirement I hope the greatest satisfaction to him will come from the love and affection of his Newcastle constituents, whom he served unstintingly, and from the warmth of feelings flowing from a vast community of loyal friends – in politics, the law and beyond.

Joyce Quinn

"I have happy memories of Brenda,
including her attempts as a style guru to give me advice and help
on colours, outfits and making a favourable visual impression!"

*J. H. Beecham, as Sir Toby, swaggered and blustered with élan …*

Although Jeremy's life and my own have followed quite different paths, we have always remained within sight of each other and can be described as 'friends of old'. We grew up in almost adjacent streets in Jesmond, Newcastle. We attended the same school – the Royal Grammar School – but it was obvious from a very early age that Jeremy was destined for high places. We attended the same birthday parties, were Barmitzvah in the same synagogue in Eskdale Terrace, just up the road from school, and with only a couple of years between us we were familiar with the same people, young and old. As now, he was an avid reader; he absorbed history like a sponge, especially political history, although he was able to see the comic side of life. An early fan of *Hancock's Half Hour*, Jeremy was able to grasp the tragicomic side of the main character, Anthony Aloysius Hancock. I had my own name for Jeremy, *Jerome de Beauchamp*, perhaps sensing his future nobility as Baron Beecham.

Whilst most of us in our early teens were more interested in devouring the latest Eagle comic or in knocking a cricket ball around St George's Church Green in Jesmond, Jeremy had already embarked on his long and illustrious political career, joining the Labour Party in 1959 and swiftly becoming the secretary of the local branch.

It's possible to catch several glimpses of Jeremy's early brilliance by glancing through the pages of the School Magazine, *NOVO*. His name appears on the committees of numerous societies, from Classics to

Debating, History to Music, usually in the chair or as secretary. He was also an enthusiastic participant in many plays at the school theatre:

March 1959, Julius Caesar: *J. H. Beecham, as Antony, led the mob while appearing to follow it, just like a subtle advertising agent.*

April 1960, Twelfth Night: *The comic trio were nice contrasts. J. H. Beecham, as Sir Toby, swaggered and blustered with élan, but sometimes sacrificed clarity to gruffness.*

"These clothes are good enough to drink in."
Twelfth Night, Act 1 Scene 3

Never afraid of courting confrontation, a letter to the editor illustrates the early (and later) Jeremy (of the Removes):

> *As Chairman of two Middle School Societies I feel it is my duty to write in protest concerning the lack of co-operation between these Societies and their Senior counterparts. In the case of the Middle School Debating Society one would perhaps expect some degree of encouragement and interest from the 'parent' Society … The situation regarding the two History Societies is in my opinion even more deplorable. No suggestions as to the correct running of a History Society, selecting a suitable programme, or, indeed, any other advice has been forthcoming. No offer from any of the 'Great Lords' (!!) of the Upper School to lecture to the Middle School Society has been received, nor has there been the slightest suggestion with regard to admitting members of the Middle School to 'suitable' meetings of the Senior Society. It is also unfortunate that the majority of English and History masters seem to share this negative attitude … I earnestly hope that in future the more experienced and abler members of the committees of both the Debating Society and the History Society will do a great deal more to assist their Juniors, thus not only strengthening the Middle School Societies, but also providing better prospects for their own.*

> *I am, Sir, Yours sincerely, J. H. BEECHAM (R1)*

In *NOVO* of April 1962, he was congratulated on being awarded a scholarship in history at University College Oxford, where he was to win a first-class honours degree in law. Also in that issue, regarding his work with the Music Society, which also applied to his many other school 'clubs' as they are now called: *Our thanks must go, as ever, to the Vice-Presidents, and also to the Chairman, for his unflagging energy and initiative.*

A Letter from Oxford (as well as Cambridge) regularly appeared in the pages of *NOVO* and the (by then) notable alumnus Jeremy was regularly mentioned in some humorous vein:

> Jan 1964: *Mr Beecham himself has become involved in a minor scandal by applying well-practised debating society methods of electioneering to Labour Club elections.*

*May 1965: Mr Beecham, or Jeremy B as he is known, is still a man to be reckoned with in the Labour Club (though he has turned respectable recently and can even claim to have had nothing to do with the last ballot-rigging scandal).*

One can only wonder!

His climb up the Labour Party ladder came soon after he returned to Newcastle to practise Law:  Jeremy began his multi-marathon post as a councillor for Benwell in 1967, something which continued after he was raised to the peerage until 2022.  Few North East residents will be unaware of his extremely active council leadership, lasting 17 years from the 1970s into the 1990s. Many of his political and charitable activities will be well noted elsewhere in this book, as well as in the Parallel Parliament website[1], but it was the chairmanship of the Local Government Association that led to his knighthood in 1994 and his subsequent rise to the peerage in July 2010.

With the proliferation of online streaming and recordings it was possible to see him in his robes during the inauguration. After his introduction he took the oath, supported by Lord Walton of Detchant and Lord Cunningham of Felling. It was an amazingly proud day for his family. Brenda, the daughter of our family doctor, Sammy Woolf, had been Jeremy's childhood sweetheart. They married in 1968, and apart from (probably, had it happened) eschewing the life of a parliamentary spouse, she supported Jeremy throughout his long political career. When his one and only attempt at becoming an MP – standing against the formidable Dame Irene Ward in Tynemouth in 1970 – was unsuccessful, Brenda was not too disappointed.

Brenda was a strong supporter of the State of Israel, but like Jeremy she wanted the state to realise the ideals of its founders, not least in relation to the rights of its Arab minority, and to withdraw from the settlements. After her untimely death in September 2010, Jeremy himself wrote

1. www.parallelparliament.co.uk/lord/lord-beecham

in an obituary, "She also supported, not without occasional justifiable resentment, my consuming interest in politics and, despite periodically threatening never to vote Labour again during the last 13 years, she always did". Likewise, Jeremy supported Brenda in her untiring efforts in aid of the Campaign for Soviet Jewry, the international human rights campaign advocating the right to emigrate of Jews in the Soviet Union.

On the personal side, I will always recall with amusement and great pleasure accompanying him on a trip to Paris in 1964 with his close neighbour and friend Anthony (Tony) Book, later to be his best man, and my cousin Daniel Goldwater, whose premises in Collingwood Street Jeremy's legal practice, *Beecham Peacock,* took over after Daniel moved to London.

Jeremy, David, Tony and Daniel in Paris, 1964

We stayed in a Jewish students' hostel named *Le Toit Familial*, where, to our amusement, the administrators struggled over Jeremy's middle name, Hugh: 'Hoog?' Tony and Daniel insisted on racing us across alternative routes on the Paris Metro and somehow Jeremy and I always seemed to win, greeting our foes with scorn as they sprinted breathlessly into sight. Jeremy's sardonic wit was already well developed and was much in evidence throughout his political career from Newcastle City Council proceedings to House of Lords debates.

As a young councillor, in 1961 he gave me and his brother-in-law, Ian Woolf, a conducted tour around the spanking new Civic Centre in Newcastle. He was obviously very much at home there and a memorable photo of him at the end of a large committee table is a foretaste of his illustrious future.

Jeremy is brilliantly supported by his son Richard and daughter Sara. At the time of writing, despite recent infirmity, he takes a lively interest in current affairs, reading, engaging with visitors and keeping in touch with old friends. Long may it last!

David Goldwater

*Jeremy, valued friend and connoisseur of jokes …*

I have known Jeremy for over 45 years. Our friendship began through my meeting his wonderful wife, Brenda. She was my post-natal visitor (a brilliant scheme set up by the NCT in our local area, where mums who were just a few months further into the parenthood lark would visit those with very new babies) and called at my home when our firstborn was only five or six weeks old. Baby Henry had colic and – as so many new parents can testify – the crying that accompanies the tummy pains in babies with colic can wreck a previously calm and reasonably efficient household. Brenda (a health visitor in a previous life) said she "had the solution" and rushed off to the chemist to purchase some colic medicine. It worked … or Henry grew out of his colic (we'll never know). However, the medicine was later banned for such young babies! That was the beginning of a long, humorous and rewarding friendship with both Brenda and Jeremy.

Brenda and I undertook the NCT ante-natal training programme together in the 1980s. This period involved a fair amount of 'studying' together in each other's homes. It was during these sessions (often over rather good lunches) that Jeremy came to refer to me as his "favourite voluntary body". His humour and wit were always apparent and we came to expect at least one joke from either of us at each meeting. Brenda, like Jeremy, saw the funny side of what were often difficult and challenging encounters. Breaking ice, reaching out – however 'putting people at their ease' can be expressed metaphorically – they were the best at making people feel at ease and welcome. I remember telling Jeremy about a recent 'Parenthood Education' session Brenda and I had facilitated in a local secondary school. As all good teachers do, we had made our own resources for explaining the female reproductive organs. Shelled almonds were the perfect substitute for the ovaries together with appropriately cut pieces of string for the fallopian tubes. I was to start the session and soon reached for the almond ovaries to find that they weren't where I'd put them. Somewhat puzzled, I turned to Brenda … who was eating them! As an ice breaker in a potentially testing lesson it worked brilliantly. When I told Jeremy he wasn't at all surprised. Like him, Brenda loved almonds!

As a mature student I wanted to enrol on a BSc Hons programme at (the then) Newcastle Polytechnic. In order to be accepted I needed two references. Jeremy gladly agreed to be one of my referees. I have no idea what he wrote, but I duly entered the course. I was surprised to be invited to the Head of Department's office a few weeks after I enrolled, and was greeted by three august senior (male) academics. They asked me how I was coping and we chatted rather superficially about the subjects with which I was getting to grips. It turned out that what they really wanted to discuss was how I had managed to secure a reference from the well-respected Leader of the Council – one Jeremy Beecham. Of course I simply told them I was his "favourite voluntary body"!

Both Brenda and Jeremy were excellent dinner party guests and hosts. We have many memories of laughing until we cried over silly jokes, great wit and satire. I can't write a brief memoir without including one of Jeremy's excellent jokes. Reading can never replace the quiet, anticipatory way it was told, but here goes:

The Chicken Soup Joke: A man went into a very posh New York restaurant. He was greeted warmly and shown to his table. The waiter presented a menu and said, 'Sir, I can highly recommend the chicken soup'. The customer replied that he'd heard the soup was excellent and would indeed order some. The chicken soup duly came and was presented with great flair. A few minutes later the customer signalled to the waiter.

'I'm not satisfied; please taste the soup.'    'Oh, Sir,' the waiter replied, 'there is absolutely no need; this soup is the very best there is'. He walked away. Some moments later, the customer again hailed the waiter. 'Please send the head waiter, I need him to taste the soup.'    Rather belligerently the waiter went and fetched the head waiter. When he arrived at the table he was asked to 'taste the soup' by the customer. 'Sir, I can assure you that our chicken soup has won many awards. Nobody has ever complained about the taste; there is no need to taste the soup.'    The customer, very indignant now, demanded that the manager be called. The head man arrived and rather patronisingly bent over the table and looked at the offending bowl of broth. 'Now, Sir,' he said with a slight smirk, 'you will never taste a better, more fragrant chicken soup'. 'You taste it, then,' said the customer.  With an audience of other diners now totally engaged with the proceedings, the manager agreed to taste the soup and reached for the spoon. 'Where is the spoon?' he asked.  'Aha!' proclaimed the exonerated customer!

Jeremy has always had the rare skill and ability of being able to welcome and relate to people from all walks of life. I have never witnessed anything remotely like bragging or immodest behaviour throughout our friendship. He sensitively attended the funerals of my late brother and father, even though they were unknown to him. Jeremy's sense of care, duty and compassion are part of who he is.

He loves Geordie humour and is totally at home watching 'the match' as a passionate supporter of the Toon – Newcastle's football team.  Equally, he has always enjoyed theatre and film.  We've often arranged, with other friends, trips to the wonderful Tyneside Cinema. These outings became particularly important after Brenda died. Jeremy would often drive my husband and me in his car and we would park in the Civic Centre – being a councillor afforded a few perks – from where we could walk, often arm in arm, the half mile to the cinema.  As long as I had Clarnico peppermint creams Jeremy would sit next to me! Many a time afterwards we would go to Wagamama for supper, to discuss the film or (more likely) to lament the Toon's recent performance.

We've all benefitted from his love of books. Birthdays and Christmas have been times for cleverly chosen texts. I have Jeremy to thank for introducing me to some brilliant writers: Italo Calvino, Amos Oz, Hilary Mantel and William Boyd, to name a diverse few. I also remember a 60th birthday gift of the extremely funny (a certain kind of humour which I share with Jeremy) box set of 'Curb your Enthusiasm'. In return, my gifts to Jeremy are nearly always of the culinary kind. He loves, in particular, my bramble mousse and fruit cake. I recall him accepting one Christmas cake saying, "A fruit cake, from a fruit cake, to a fruit cake!" He's always been something of a chef himself, and over the years we have often enjoyed his excellent Moroccan chicken and lamb tagine.

Jeremy, Knight and Lord of the Realm, may have been rightly rewarded for his services to local and national government, but to me and my husband Gavin he'll always be a very lovely, loyal friend whose wit, intelligence and humour need no such accolades.

Gavin adds:

I could not agree more. Like Joan, my friendship with Jeremy came via Brenda; my professional relationship with Jeremy came about later in the Central Magistrates Courts on Market Street. I had been appointed to the prosecutions department of Northumbria Police which dealt with all criminal cases brought by the police in the Newcastle district. On Mondays and Wednesdays, I would represent the police in Court One, in what were called *Plea or Adjourn* cases. Persons accused of minor to major offences made their first court appearance on these days and could enter a plea of guilty to minor offences, such as drunkenness, or find their cases adjourned to a later date with bail conditions set by the court.

Jeremy regularly used to appear in these courts representing miscreants of all shapes and sizes. We each played our part, although I do recall with some embarrassment one minor case when Jeremy's client changed his plea to 'not guilty' of being drunk and disorderly. The magistrates agreed with Jeremy's request for them to hear the case there and then, as we had come to the end of the list of cases and he had a lot of council business to do. Suddenly I found I was expected to act the lawyer and conduct the prosecution. I stumbled through this as the novice I was. Jeremy got a fit of giggles and ended up prompting me with questions I should ask his client. The magistrate's clerk was also having difficulty in keeping a straight face, and quietly suggested to the magistrates a reduction of the charge to one of simple drunkenness, with a minor fine.

Joan, Brenda, Jeremy and Gavin with the bird table
that the practical Gavin built for the Beechams.

Jeremy has many talents, but practical DIY is not one of them – he relies on others for those mundane tasks. A very funny incident happened one Sunday morning, when Brenda called me to seek my help. She explained that there was a strong, foul smell permeating the house and the kitchen sink was blocked. I listened to her then responded, "But Brenda, why are you asking me?" Straight away she came back, "Well you are studying an environmental degree aren't you? You should know about dead rats". I went along, to find Jeremy there, quietly chuckling and demanding that I should do my duty. I failed to find any rats, but with a certain inventor pal of his we did manage to clean out the macerator under the sink. Jeremy's penchant for bunging all sorts of stuff down it was to blame – said Brenda!

It is Jeremy's sense of humour and fun that have always endeared him to me. He loves tales of my police experience, especially those that are a bit naughty. Once, at a dinner party at our home, I recall Jeremy laughing so much when I told the company about how one evening a young boy came into North Shields Police Station with a small, aged dog and explained to the constable at the desk that he'd found it in the street. There was no collar, no identification. In those days – I hope things have changed – stray pets had to be taken to the cat and dog shelter on Claremont Road in Newcastle, which meant losing a vehicle and driver for at least an hour for such a trip from North Shields. On this occasion, the officer assessed the sad state of the little moth-eaten pooch, took it into a back room and put it into a small humane killer usually used for injured pigeons and the like. He poured a dose of chloroform into the cage and left the dog to perish quietly. He had no sooner resumed his post at the front desk than an elderly lady entered and said, "Little Johnny from down the road has just telt me he brought Fido in here". Panic! The officer rushed back, yanked the comatose Fido out of the death-cage and held it under a cold tap in the sink. Still quite wet, Fido was taken out and placed on the desk in front of the inquirer, who immediately identified it as her dog … but wondered why it couldn't stand and was so wet. The officer explained it had been caught in a very localised heavy shower and was rather tired. Situation saved.

Joan and Gavin Aarvold

*Jeremy is the kind of person*
*you want to be in charge of local government …*

I first encountered Jeremy Beecham in the early 1970s when I was a secretary of the Elswick Action Centre, a campaigning group of local people in Newcastle's West End, which at the time was a slum clearance area. He was a young solicitor, known to campaign groups as a friendly lawyer who would give free advice over the phone and help to ensure fair treatment at the hands of the police. A couple of incidents were typical:

On one occasion a boy of 14 was suspected of theft and arrested by the police. The action group ran a scheme for young people and the boy was known to be one of the least likely to commit crimes. He was innocent but was held by the police for questioning. As a child he should have been questioned in the presence of one of his parents, who lived around ten minutes from the police station. I rang Jeremy Beecham for advice before going to the police station on behalf of the mother. Initially they pretended that they had acted within the law, but when I pointed out that I had spoken to Jeremy they conceded that a parent should have been present. Jeremy provided free advice to anyone in similar circumstances.

On another occasion he defended in the magistrate's court an activist who had been arrested by the police for blocking a road. The Elswick Action Centre was campaigning for a zebra crossing on a route to the local school and on one morning a group of about twenty mothers blocked the road, calling upon the council to provide a safe crossing. The police arrived and agreed with the leaders of the protest that the road could be blocked for another 15 minutes, then everyone must move. Everyone agreed except a couple of extreme-left hotheads who had attached themselves to the protest. They took the view that agreeing to end the blockade was an act of treason against the working class; they would have no truck with 'class collaboration'. They were given a final warning and then arrested and charged. Jeremy defended one of the accused. Jeremy was no radical and probably disapproved of direct action, but he believed that the law should be enforced fairly.

I ran into him again when I was a city councillor from 1976 until moving to Australia in 1981. He was Leader of the City Council towards the end of that period. At the time the Labour Party in Newcastle was much troubled by the Militant Tendency and Jeremy was a determined opponent of their extremism.

He was a leader known for his straight dealing. He was not ostentatious, but was hard-working and in command of policy detail. One incident was typical. A voter in my ward told me that he had gone to the housing department to get permission to make changes to his house. The council would usually approve such changes as long as its staff prepared the official plans for any building work. The charge was around £150, but council officials were in the habit of offering to do the work for about half the price. They were doing this during working hours and the council was losing revenue. I was the vice-chairman of the housing management committee and raised the problem with the chairman and with Jeremy as Leader of the City Council.

I suspect that many leaders would have turned a blind eye because the officials denied everything and the witness didn't want any trouble. Jeremy handled it by telling the officials that the council knew what was happening, but that if it stopped immediately no further action would be taken. It stopped.

I moved way from the North East and had no contact with Jeremy for over 30 years until 2013, when we bought a flat in Newcastle. I renewed an old friendship with another former Labour councillor and he invited Jeremy to dinner. We met at our flat before going on to the restaurant. As it happened, the City Council was trying to charge us more than the normal rate of council tax because it claimed the flat was empty, when in fact we were regularly in residence. I mentioned the problem in passing to Jeremy and he took it up with the relevant chief officer in writing and on the phone. We were not in his ward and did not ask for help, but he did not like to see the council acting unfairly, and he put them straight.

In a cynical age it is difficult to praise a genuinely good person without sounding pretentious or even a bit sanctimonious, but Jeremy is the kind of person you want to be in charge of local government. His sense of duty made him a hard worker, his strong conscience would not let him knowingly do wrong, and he had an ingrained sense of justice.

David Green

Knight Bachelor
honour conferred by Her Majesty the Queen
22 November 1994.

*Irrespective of class, colour, religion or ethnic origin …*

Ifirst met Lord Beecham when I moved to Newcastle to take up my post as Director of the Tyne & Wear Racial Equality Council (REC) in 1974; the newly formed REC was being reorganised and Jeremy was Leader of Newcastle City Council. Jeremy played a very important role in helping the REC to lay a strong foundation for good community relations in Tyne & Wear, establishing an 'open door' policy from the very beginning, and welcoming members from the ethnic minority communities to discuss their issues. Jeremy was convinced that the best way to resolve any problems was by having open and honest conversations about issues that mattered the most. He believed that a multi-cultural society was an asset and brought vibrancy to our communities, and that every individual – irrespective of his or her background – has a role to play in contributing to the welfare of the wider community.

In the early days there was little or no contact between the diverse groups, but Jeremy worked tirelessly to help them come together and work for the benefit of the whole locality. Within a few years, all of the communities had begun to co-operate and to make a positive contribution to the economic, social and cultural life of the region. Jeremy holds strong Jewish traditions and values but has tremendous respect for the many other cultures and faiths that make up the fabric of our society. His leadership was pivotal in creating an atmosphere of unity and peace, where people of all faiths – and none – could work together. He was highly respected by all of the various communities and was invited by the Sikh Community to officially open the newly-built Sikh Gurdwara. This was followed by an invitation to open the new mosque, built by the Muslim community.

Jeremy with members of the Sikh community in the 1970s.

During my 35 years as Director of the Tyne & Wear REC, Jeremy acted as my mentor and provided invaluable advice when I was dealing with sensitive issues. Ours became one of the leading RECs in the country, with Jeremy's leadership crucial to our success. In the first ten years people gained the confidence to establish their own businesses and today members of ethnic minority communities are successfully developing and diversifying their many enterprises.

We enjoy peace and harmony in our region. Third and fourth generations are playing a fitting role in the life of the communities, and the foundations for this success are testimony to Jeremy's hard work and commitment … his vision for a cohesive society. Following his elevation to the House of Lords, Jeremy continued to take an interest in the life of the North East and is considered by diverse communities to be the leader who was instrumental in building bridges amongst different groups, resulting in the unity that we enjoy today. People continue to be inspired by Jeremy's wise counsel and leadership.

Jeremy has a passion for service that benefits the whole community, particularly those that are vulnerable, the most disadvantaged and marginalised sections of our society. He is recognised as a man of exceptional talent for winning people round, and for straightening out differences whilst successfully carrying out a leading role in an important organisation such as the local authority. His zeal, his exceptional foresight and sincerity together with tenacity and determination paved the way for creating partnerships and understanding amongst people, irrespective of their class, colour, religion or ethnic origin.

Our region is multifaith, and Jeremy strongly believes that in order to have a successful multifaith society it is essential to have an understanding about the traditions that different faiths hold. With this in mind, he encouraged communities to share their values and principles with other people. Aware of the fact that all religions celebrate festivals, he encouraged people to invite others from diverse faith communities to join them in celebration. In time, people from very different communities began to support one another as they learned and understood each other's values; this led to a growing respect for one another. Interfaith relationships improved and people began to enjoy harmonious community relations. People began to work together and friendships developed; Jeremy was the catalyst for these improved relations. Despite his very busy diary, he made time to promote links and friendships between our communities.

Conscious of the fact that it was essential for children to be enlightened about other faiths, Jeremy made sure that the City Council developed a policy to help schools establish comprehensive religious studies syllabuses. At the same time, it was realised that teachers needed help and support to teach religious education in a meaningful way, so with the help of our communities, the council set about gathering instructive material on each of the main religious traditions for school use. When these were ready, Jeremy convened a meeting – which he chaired – to confirm these guidelines, after which they proved to be greatly beneficial to the schools.

In order to tackle inequality, Jeremy realised that it was important for all the major institutions to develop policies to address discrimination and promote equal opportunities. He convened a meeting with the major institutions, including those from higher and further education, the police, criminal justice organisations, the CBI, TUC and the Chamber of Commerce. This was the beginning of the development of a strong partnership to address racial issues and to challenge inequality. Jeremy's leadership was recognised by Newcastle University, when he was awarded an honorary doctorate. His wise leadership was greatly appreciated by people at a national level: he was elected President of the Local Government Association and served with distinction for many years.

Jeremy with Mr and Mrs Hari Shukla

Jeremy was my mentor. He supported me in my work as Director of Tyne & Wear Racial Equality Council for twenty years, until I retired. Today our region enjoys good community relations as a result of Jeremy's hard work, dedication, wise leadership and selflessness, for which we are indebted to him.

Hari Shukla

# Benwell and the Toon

On his retirement, Jeremy's ward colleagues, Hazel Stephenson and Rob Higgins, stated: "His dedication to serving our community is legendary; there isn't a family he hasn't helped, or a local community group he hasn't supported."

*"Have you met God? Well, he's up there now."*

I first met Jeremy Beecham in the Spring of 1974. This was a significant year in both national and local politics. In February, in the midst of a worsening economic situation and volatile industrial relations, the then Prime Minister, Edward Heath, had held a general election, focusing on the question, "Who governs Britain?". The outcome was a victory for the Labour Party which formed a minority government, later gaining a majority in a second election eight months later. One of Heath's most important acts had been a major restructuring of local government in England and Wales involving, among other innovations, a two-tier system of metropolitan districts covering mainly urban areas and metropolitan counties which brought together groups of districts. A new county of Tyne and Wear was created, with the hitherto unimaginable consequence of bringing together in a single organisation the historic rivals of Newcastle and Sunderland. At the district council level, the city of Newcastle upon Tyne was considerably enlarged, taking in the semi-rural former coalmining areas to the west and north of the existing boundary as well as the largely middle-class suburb of Gosforth. This changed the demographic profile of Newcastle, with implications for its politics. In the local elections held in 1973, the Labour Party won a majority after almost a decade of Conservative dominance of Newcastle Council. However, Labour did not actually take control until the following year, operating in the meantime as a 'shadow council' – an arrangement which afforded the opportunity to develop detailed plans and policies before getting caught up in the practical details of implementation. April 1974 was therefore an exciting time for the city, with a new leadership armed with new ideas and a determination to improve the quality of life after years of stagnation. Although not the leader at that stage, Jeremy was a key player in the new regime. His particular passion was social services in the broadest sense, and his achievements included the development of a welfare rights service and increased support for the voluntary sector.

**About Your Labour Candidate**

Jeremy Beecham is a 25 year old City Solicitor. His wife is a nurse.

Educated in Newcastle and Oxford University where he gained a First Class Honours Degree in Law and was Chairman of the Labour Club.

Joined the Labour Party in 1959, is Vice-Chairman of Newcastle North C.L.P., Secretary of the Council Labour Group and Prospective Labour Candidate for Tynemouth in the General Election.

Elected Councillor for Benwell Ward in 1967; has served on the Finance, Health, Traffic, Arts, Library, General Purposes and Housing Management Committees.

Member of the Clerical Workers Union, Newcastle and Gateshead Trades Council, Community Relations Council, Child Poverty Action Group, Disablement Income Group Fabian Society and the Society of Labour Lawyers.

Director of Tyneside Theatre Trust and Vice-Chairman of the Friends of the Theatre Royal.

Has Lectured on Industrial Law.

Special interests are housing, welfare services and recreation.

**Ardent campaigner for Benwell and its people.**

**Beecham for Benwell**

# vote labour

on
**Thursday, May 7th**          8 a.m. — 9 p.m.

| BEECHAM | X |

Published by Doris Starkey, 13, Victoria Square, Newcastle, NE2 4DD, and printed by Co-operative Printing Society Ltd., Rutherford Street, Newcastle upon Tyne.

By the time I arrived in Benwell in 1974, Jeremy had already been a councillor for the ward since 1967. An early influence had been his fellow councillor Connie Lewcock, who had played an important role in tackling the city's massive housing problems during the 1960s under the leadership of T. Dan Smith. She had been a radical suffragette in her early years, even confessing towards the end of her life to acts of arson – but Jeremy, who had no revolutionary inclinations, was happily unaware of this. What they did share was a deep concern about the appalling housing conditions endured by many local residents and a determination to tackle its manifest social problems. Jeremy's devotion to Benwell, and his capacity to be personally moved by its problems, never wavered throughout the 55 years during which he continuously served as ward councillor.

I had returned to Tyneside in 1974, after five years' absence, to work for the National Community Development Project – Britain's first and only ever national anti-poverty programme. Benwell had been chosen as the location of one of the CDP's twelve experimental projects. This was the first time that the area was officially labelled as 'deprived'. Our remit was to research the causes of poverty, develop measures to tackle it, and evaluate the effectiveness of these. Although I was employed by Durham University as part of the research team, we were all based in premises in the heart of Benwell and took responsibility for both research and action. Benwell CDP had its critics on the City Council. The then Conservative-led council had accepted the project with little thought about the implications, perhaps assuming that any problems would only affect Labour-held wards in parts of the city at a safe distance from Conservative areas. Once it was underway, some aspects of the work prompted outrage from a number of Conservative councillors who saw the project as dangerously radical and staffed by trouble-makers. During debates in the council chamber, Jeremy derived great enjoyment from mocking his opponents for their lack of understanding of the realities of life in areas like Benwell in comparison with the leafy suburbs they represented.

Perhaps more surprisingly, there were also critics from within the Labour group, including some councillors in adjacent wards, who resented the intrusion of paid outsiders into what they considered to be their role. One Elswick councillor complained, "We don't need these bookish people" – a comment which struck me as odd considering that she was a school teacher. Meanwhile Jeremy, in whose ward we were based, maintained a supportive and amicable relationship with the project throughout its five years. The potential for conflict was built into the CDP model, as the remit would almost inevitably lead to criticism of local authority policies and services – notably in the field of housing at a time when council housing was the dominant tenure locally. In practice, several of the CDP projects in other parts of the country fell out badly with their host councils, to the extent that some were closed down prematurely. This did not happen in Newcastle, probably owing largely to Jeremy's support. His view was that the ward benefited from the additional resources and the encouragement of community activism, no matter how uncomfortable this might make his life as a councillor. In fact, contrary to the situation in most other places where councils were only too pleased to wave goodbye to the troublesome CDPs, the 'action' elements of the Benwell project were taken on by Newcastle Council at the end of the project with the creation of a community resource centre staffed by the former CDP workers.

During this period I also lived in Benwell, and became an active member of the local Labour Party, as did some of my CDP colleagues. This might look at first sight to be part of the explanation for Jeremy's support of the project, but in reality it was yet another potential source of conflict. The Labour Party in the mid-1970s was riven by serious debates about the direction of national policy, especially as it affected the relationship between government and industry. These debates were particularly relevant to Benwell which was undergoing an accelerating process of deindustrialisation. I was on the left of the Party, as were most of my friends and colleagues, although none of us belonged to the leadership's bête noire – the Militant Tendency.[1] Jeremy's views favoured the Croslandite wing of the Party, and we considered him an unreconstructed social democrat, holding back the march of progress

1. For the record, nor were we later connected to Momentum.

towards socialism. Despite this, we all got along very well and there was no personal animosity.

Election campaigns were a time to dread. Jeremy was unstoppable. I think we were the only branch who had to canvass every evening without a night off on a Friday. Jeremy was incurably bossy – preferring to stand in the middle of the road shouting orders to his troops – "Number 82, Mr and Mrs Brown!" and so on. One of my enduring memories is meeting the late Arthur Stabler, councillor of the next ward of West City, storming out of the Benwell committee rooms during a general election campaign shouting to me, "Have you met God? Well, he's up there now". The other source of discomfort at election time was the literature, which Jeremy would write and which would be peppered with the terrible puns of which he was so fond. I have to confess that I once punched Jeremy in the guts in a fit of irritation after a particularly arduous campaign. I'm not sure if the whiskies I had imbibed in the Crows Nest in Benwell as we tried to wind down provide an excuse for this offence or make it worse. Jeremy, of course, never over-indulged. His self-control was legendary: his fellow councillor Walter Wilson once remarked to me as Jeremy left the room, "I'd love to get that man drunk". I discovered later when I worked for the City Council that housing officers and other council staff dreaded election times, as Jeremy would inundate them daily with dozens of curt memos about cracked pavements, broken street lights and all the other minor problems he noted as he canvassed every street in Benwell.

One of the achievements of which Jeremy was most proud was the establishment of the Priority Areas Project in the 1970s. This was a ward-based project which targeted the poorest neighbourhoods in the city, giving them a substantial budget to spend in the area and a dedicated officer known as a Priority Area Team Leader to manage the budget and service the team. Initially the 'team' was envisaged as comprising the elected councillors for that ward, council officers from different service areas, and representatives of community organisations, who would meet regularly to discuss local problems and identify appropriate spending measures, but it soon shifted into a system of public meetings taking place within each area. The project was Jeremy's personal brainchild, and it aimed to improve the quality of life in the poorest areas in a number of ways. The budget enabled projects to be funded in response to locally identified needs, and money could be spent flexibly and promptly as required. It helped to hold council officers to account by the communities they were meant to be serving, and to shape services to fit local circumstances. It brought individual councillors closer to the residents they served, supplementing surgeries and other means of contact. There was also an ambition that the project could be a way of 'bending' mainline services so that the poorest areas with the greatest needs would benefit from more and better service delivery. To try to ensure that the meetings would be more than talking shops, the project was structurally integrated into the formal committee system. Each ward Priority Area was officially a council sub-committee, with a right to send recommendations and requests to other council committees which had to be placed on the relevant meeting agendas, and each local meeting was serviced by committee clerks, giving the proceedings a legal status. The project was located within the Chief Executive's department, rather than a service department, which gave it independence. and this status was reinforced by the absence of the usual hierarchical management structure above the team leaders. There was a project coordinator who gave support and coordination to the team leaders, but effectively they were accountable to their local councillors, for better or worse. The Priority Areas Project survived more or less in this form for a couple of decades before being diluted in various ways. It is worth focusing on here because it illustrates not only Jeremy's relationship with his ward and his modus operandi, but also his enduring commitment to tackling poverty and inequality and to improving public services.

I worked as the Benwell Priority Area Team Leader from 1983 for almost ten years. At that time, team leaders were appointed by the councillors for each particular ward. The fact that I was employed for Benwell after having been for years an independent, and often critical, community worker at the CDP and later the Law Project is in itself an indication of the role that I was expected to fulfil. This was suggested during the recruitment stage when the shortlisted candidates were taken out to a Benwell team meeting to observe the proceedings. In response to concerns raised by residents in one part of the ward, Jeremy stated that one of the first tasks for the successful candidate would be to help set up a residents association. They were evidently not looking for a bag carrier.

Our Benwell meetings took place every month on a Tuesday evening. Bear in mind that Jeremy at this time, in addition to being leader of a council staggering under the onslaught of hostile Conservative policies as well as the disintegration of the city's industrial infrastructure, was an important actor on the wider stage, including being the most important figure in local government nationally. Prioritising his ward, he never missed a PAT meeting. On time to the exact minute, he would rush into whatever community centre or school hall we were meeting in that month – probably having just come off a train from London having chaired a meeting of the Local Government Association or met with a government minister. When I once asked him what I should do if he didn't arrive for a PAT meeting, he replied that he always would. In fact, on one occasion no councillors had appeared by ten minutes past the starting time. Faced with a room full of increasingly restless residents, I decided that we had to go ahead with the meeting even if no decisions could be taken in the absence of any councillors. Fortunately, Jeremy swept in 15 minutes late, sat down, grabbed the papers from me, and took over the meeting without drawing breath.

Jeremy chaired every meeting, and he was an amazing chair. We always had substantial agendas, including local issues, reports from departments and local organisations, as well as the grant-giving process. Although the Benwell agendas were considerably longer than those of any other team, the meetings never lasted more than an hour and a half. To me it felt like half a lifetime, as we covered so many issues and I had to be ready to respond to unexpected questions on just about any subject. Some of my colleagues had to endure meetings that dragged on for several hours, but ours always ended promptly. Somehow Jeremy had an ability to get through a large amount of business while allowing every local resident to have a say. Nor did he use the meetings as a platform to hold forth about his own achievements and opinions. He was also very funny, lightening the proceedings with jokes – and those bad puns again. Other local workers likened it to a stand-up comedy performance. My role as lead officer was to sit next to him, and he had a disconcerting habit of muttering comments in my ear or passing me messages in his barely readable scrawl while different speakers were talking, sometimes wanting instant answers to questions and sometimes cracking jokes. Apart from the problem of trying not to laugh (I still remember the visit of Mr Fox, the council's official dogcatcher), I found it difficult to concentrate on what was being said, but Jeremy seemed to be able to do both at the same time and would come in with sharp and pertinent questions as soon as the speaker had finished.

Priority Area Team meetings could be very unpleasant experiences for council officers, as some councillors were prone to abuse and humiliate officers in an effort to demonstrate their power and show local residents that they were acting forcefully in their interests. This never happened in Benwell PAT meetings. Jeremy treated everyone with respect, even if he did insist that council officers provide answers. My job was to pressure officers behind the scenes not to set them up for a public trial, and to extract information and agreements from different departments. Never having worked in local government previously and being unaccustomed to hierarchical structures and deferential behaviour, I didn't find this too difficult, and being the representative of the Leader of the Council gave me a certain clout. Part of my job involved writing memos to officers in Jeremy's name at his behest – although I suspect people could differentiate between my carefully crafted paragraphs and his minimalist messages which rarely extended beyond one sentence.

I found it quite strange when I first entered the world of the Civic

Centre.  So many people addressed Jeremy as 'Leader' (which used to remind me of a scene from Star Trek)  and bowed and scraped – far from how we were used to treating him in Benwell.  It was not uncommon to come out of a meeting in his office with a group of senior officers to be asked, "What did he mean?"  I couldn't understand why they didn't just ask him as I did when he mumbled some cryptic comment, but he seemed to instil fear and anxiety in the most unlikely people.  When I told Jeremy this years later, he was horrified.

The public meetings in Benwell were always friendly affairs.  An indication of the atmosphere fostered by Jeremy's chairmanship was on the occasion soon after he was knighted when an officer referred to him as "Sir Jeremy", and he interrupted to say, "I am just Jeremy here".

Jeremy at the official
opening ceremony of
South Benwell Primary School
in 1981.

Local residents were listened to with respect and their concerns, however trivial they might appear to others, were treated sympathetically.  Jeremy was not in the business of currying favour, however.  He was very clear that decisions had to be taken, and there were often difficult choices to be made which could result in some people losing out. He never pretended to support a local objection if he didn't believe in it, or to divert the blame for a council policy or plan onto someone else if he himself supported it. For him, the meetings were an arena for genuine discussion and exchange of views, even if you couldn't please everyone at the end of the day. In my experience, Jeremy is a pluralist in his approach – by which I mean, in the local context, that he considered that people not only have the right to oppose and to campaign against council decisions but also to be given resources and support for this purpose. In this respect, he differed markedly from some Newcastle councillors I have known who regarded themselves as much more progressive than Jeremy but were in practice rather authoritarian when they met active opposition from local people to their own plans and policies. I would go further and say that he was a more assiduous local councillor than many who derided him. In all those decades he never lost his interest in even the most mundane details, and his concern for Benwell remains undimmed even after his retirement.

The grant-giving function was an important aspect of the PAT's work. My role was to support local groups and organisations to develop solid funding bids for activities and projects of benefit to the area, to ensure that the councillors had adequate information on which to take decisions, and to evaluate and report back afterwards. It is hard to believe now but, in those days, the grant application forms were very brief, asking for little more than what the project or activity was and how much money was requested. Jeremy was unusual in taking a more business-like approach. He expected a high level of background information to support grant applications. For example, for bids from organisations working across more than one ward, he would require evidence of how many people were Benwell residents. It was my job to obtain this information – often prompting objections from organisations who thought this was unreasonable, since none of the other PATs asked for it. If I put together a detailed evidence-based case for or against a grant, my advice was almost always followed, and there was never any hint of favouritism in the decision-making. Occasionally Jeremy would veto a bid, but this was so rare that I can only recall one specific example. This was an application for an event in Benwell from an organisation which Jeremy considered to be political (not in the party-political sense). He wouldn't discuss it, just flatly said no. I suspect that, in the turbulent political context of the period, he was wary that it might risk tainting Newcastle with the accusation of being a 'loony left' council. A week or so later, I had an opportunity to wreak revenge for this rejection of my excellent advice. A worker from Search, a local organisation working with older people, mentioned that she would like to submit a grant application on behalf of a 'music and movement' group. Those who know Jeremy well will confirm that he has always had a short attention span, so I invited the group to do a demonstration. At the appropriate point in the agenda, as Jeremy was rattling through the applications giving quickfire decisions, I intervened and announced that the group had come to give a demonstration of their keep-fit activities. Jeremy hissed in my ear, "I hope you're joking!" but had to sit with a fixed smile through a performance of movement to music with much waving of colourful scarves. To his credit, he was charming to the group and awarded the full grant.

Benwell PAT produced regular newsletters which were delivered direct to local residents. At an early stage Jeremy told me that he didn't want our newsletter to look like a glossy planning handout. I was very happy with that, and produced basic leaflets every month, with additional ones for particular neighbourhoods affected by significant events such as a major housing programme. The quick turnaround enabled us to communicate plans and changes promptly, as well as to publicise at short notice information from local groups and organisations, such as spare places in a local toddler group or a school fair. In many respects it resembled a community newspaper rather than an official council newsletter. Benwell was unusual in this respect. Most of my PAT colleagues hated producing the required quarterly newsletters, because their councillors expected them to be full of glossy photographs of themselves in various settings, awarding grants or otherwise doing good deeds in the local community – especially when elections were looming. Jeremy, by contrast, always refused to have his photograph in a newsletter, apart from the standard small images of local councillors that appeared on the back with contact details. He was implacable – even when I offered him the opportunity to stand at the top of a manure heap to publicise a grant we had given to Benwell Nature Park. The only exception was our Christmas edition one year when I had the idea of having the faces of all three Benwell councillors as decorations hanging off a Christmas tree on the front page. When I ran this past Jeremy, his typical reply was to ask, "Hanging?" Unfortunately, the acting Priority Areas Coordinator, who had worked in the east end of the city where such an idea would probably have led to a threat of sacking, intercepted the draft of the newsletter in the publicity office and I was summoned to be told that this could not go ahead as it was disrespectful to the Leader of the Council. I informed him that Jeremy had approved it, and that was the end of that.

I have focused on my experience of Jeremy as a local councillor during my stints working for the Community Development Project in the 1970s and the Priority Areas Project during the 1980s-1990s. In addition, I have known him in his role as a local councillor up to his retirement in 2022, as I have been involved in research, community organising and volunteering in Benwell almost continuously for nearly 50 years, and could give numerous other examples of his love for and commitment to the area. During this time, I have come to appreciate his personal kindness and generosity – aspects of his character that were often obscured by his daunting capacity to multi-task and to leap from one activity to another without apparent pause – and we are now good friends. Perhaps there is no better illustration of his devotion to the area than the fact that he chose to be Baron Beecham of Benwell when he entered the House of Lords.

Judith Green

*Jeremy was a forceful and effective speaker*
*in meetings large or small.*

When I first knew Jeremy he was Chair of Newcastle Social Services. I was Deputy Secretary, and then General Secretary, of Newcastle Council for Voluntary Service (CVS) between 1978 and 1987. Until 2013, as a consultant/adviser and administrator of charitable trusts operating in the North East of England, I followed his political career with interest and kept in touch.

As a notable member of Newcastle's Jewish community, from a young age Jeremy's instinctive, but unobtrusive, commitment to socialist values has impressed people of all faiths and political loyalties. He has been tireless in his work for his clients, for the City of Newcastle and at national level. The long period of his leadership of the City Council – through very challenging times – is an outstanding example of dedication, inevitably involving some sacrifice of personal and family interests.

Both professionally and personally I tried to support Jeremy and his aspirations. At the CVS, in my time and in the time of my successor, the late Carole Howells, we were inevitably concerned about the government's cuts to local authority finance among other constraints, and their effects on already impoverished communities and disadvantaged groups. I organised conferences of voluntary and community organisations and a delegation of representatives of the sector to meet government ministers in London, in particular those at the (then) Department of the Environment. Through the Inner City Forum, the CVS ran a campaign focused on the needs of inner-city communities. At all times, Jeremy was a forceful and effective speaker in meetings, large or small.

I felt it was important for the City Council to know that it had our support when we confronted the government. One particular encounter has 'gone down in history'. A powerful group, representing different parts of the sector, travelled to London to meet John Patten, the somewhat patrician junior minister in the Department of the Environment. Arriving late with his retinue of civil servants, Patten said he knew why we were there, but what he *really* wanted to know was why there hadn't been any riots in Newcastle (this was soon after the disturbances on the Meadow Well estate in North Tyneside). He didn't wait for an answer, telling us that the reason was that there weren't enough black people in Newcastle to riot.

A few lasting personal memories: Jeremy scurrying – he was always scurrying from his office to the Civic Centre and back. On one particular occasion I had collected Sir George Young – an Old Etonian minister known as the 'bicycling baronet' – from the Central Station to speak at a conference. Spotting Jeremy in the street, I stopped the car; I doubt that he was impressed when George Young leaned out to proclaim in aristocratic tones, "I am the minister!". Another memory: Jeremy, seen at Gosforth ASDA with Brenda one Saturday afternoon after synagogue, in front of a cabinet of newly promoted up-market ice cream, characteristically weighing up whether to indulge. Another lasting image is of Jeremy at a meeting not long after a widely and unfairly publicised breakdown, speaking impressively and very openly about the relentless demands and pressures of his public position.

At the funeral in St Mary's Roman Catholic Cathedral of Brian Roycroft, Newcastle's former Director of Social Services, Jeremy spoke movingly about his friend, colleague and fellow architect of Newcastle's Social Services Department. I believe that establishing and developing that department is the achievement of which he is most proud.

A key aspect of Newcastle Labour's policy was the recognition and proper funding of the city's voluntary and community organisations. Strategies for this were devised over many evenings in advance of coming to power in 1974, with contributions from my predecessor at the CVS, John Long, and others of the sector's stalwarts. Over time some activists undoubtedly gave Jeremy grief, but he was always convinced and consistent in his support for the sector.

I have huge respect for Jeremy's sometimes alarming intelligence, along with his exceptional commitment and, although we have not been close friends, I have great affection for his enigmatic personality. He is the only person who insists on calling me 'Terry'!

Terence Finley

An official gathering with Lord Mayor Peter Arnold at the Civic Centre
including (back row L-R) Jeremy and Brenda, John Shipley,
an unidentified guest and Jon Gower Davies.

Charles, Prince of Wales meets Jeremy and other civic leaders
during his visit to Newcastle, 9 December 1986.

*A person of real integrity and great intellect …*

I have had a working relationship with Jeremy for almost forty years, for the most part a peripheral one, but with a few more active moments. He has always struck me as a person of real integrity and great intellect, seeking the best for the community that he serves, which has made him stand out from the wider body of local political figures.

He gently tolerated my naivety when I arrived as the regional head of government departments in the NE dealing with local government, listening to my ill-considered notions as to how the region should best deploy its assets. He shook his head in dismay when I explained that Mrs Thatcher had decided to create a development corporation to tackle dereliction on the banks of the two rivers. But despite this – and the opposition of the five local authorities in the county and several of its MPs to the new institution – he determined to make the best of it, to ensure that no lasting damage was done and that the corporation spent its money, on the whole, to good effect.

Jeremy, as Leader of the Council, had begun the redevelopment process with the beginnings of the Offshore Technology Park at Walker and of what is now the Newcastle Business Park between Scotswood Road and the river. The Tyne and Wear Development Corporation, with more liberal funding, took these over, re-invested in the infrastructure and built them into successful enterprises. The major prize, however, was the Quayside itself: again, the process had begun with the commitment of the City Council and Cyril Davies, the Chief Executive, in particular, to build the Newcastle Quayside Crown Courts in magnificent style. But the remainder of the Quayside and quay walls had fallen into severe disrepair and dereliction; the area had been broken up into about 45 different land ownerships, with several using the site for scrap, and others owning sheds previously used to store asbestos. City Road itself was beginning to slip into the river. Following a public consultation, a masterplan for redevelopment prepared by Terry Farrell – in conjunction with a developer – was chosen, and a compulsory purchase order was instituted in order to assemble the site. At this point an alternative developer for part of the site appeared, with the intention of building a twelve storey tower; he purchased key portions of the site in conjunction with a national contractor with local links to enable this, and opposed the CPO. This set off a public scrap involving public bodies, opposing local councillors and MPs, and a large international company with a major base in Newcastle and small (but historic) land ownership on the quay. Eventually the matter went to court over a two-year period, reaching the House of Lords, before the CPO was eventually confirmed and the development proceeded.

During this time there were many people with competing political interests at play, attempting to take control of the situation for their own advantage and that of their supporters. In difficult circumstances Jeremy quietly and straightforwardly sought what was best for the city as a whole, supporting the corporation in the line it took, even at moments when it looked as though things might come crashing down. This led to conflict within and outside the council which he skilfully sidestepped without ever conceding what he thought was the best outcome.

As Chief Executive of the corporation this mattered to me personally, because I found myself on more than one occasion the subject of heavy criticism for supposedly corrupt dealings. Jeremy backed me strongly in subsequent enquiries, at the risk of some cost to himself, not out of personal favour to me but because he felt strongly that there should be fair play in public life. I shall avoid naming names and re-igniting old conflicts! Newcastle is not always the easiest place to do business.

The development of the Quayside is, I believe, generally regarded as a success, though happenchance played a large part in it. Work proceeded on the Newcastle side, rebuilding the Quayside with major new buildings for commercial and leisure activities – promoted largely by the private sector with public sector support – and providing wide public open space and riverside walkways. Meanwhile, over on the Gateshead side, George Gill, the leader (Gateshead having chosen to stay out of the territory of the development corporation) was beginning to promote an Arts regeneration strategy using the finance now available from the Arts and Millennium lottery to build the Sage Concert Hall and the Baltic Art Gallery, together with the Millennium Bridge. This successfully complemented the dramatic transformation taking place on the north bank. For me, the renewal of both banks constitutes one of the finest river bank set-piece redevelopments in the UK.

Alastair, Jeremy and the Tyne God celebrate the completion of the Quayside development in 1996.

Jeremy was a little more sceptical about the development of the International Centre for Life next to Central Station, also pioneered by the development corporation. This was, and is, a science village linked to Newcastle University, building on the emergence of Genetics and DNA as major medical and scientific forces in and around the time of the millennium. It was designed not only to attract world class scientists but also to make this new world of science developing in our city, which is transforming our understanding, available to a wider public, to families in particular, just as occurred in a similar fashion at the time of major industrial innovations in Newcastle in the 19th century. After 25 years this institution is still going strong and is continuing to make its mark in many fields in the UK and more widely. I hope Jeremy's initial scepticism has been laid to rest. Jeremy has always had a great interest in the Arts as well as being an ardent follower of Newcastle United. He enjoyed the annual series of plays put on at the Theatre Royal by the Royal Shakespeare Company and was dismayed when they came to an end. He particularly wanted Newcastle, as the capital of the region, to give a lead in theatre and music.

Jeremy has never been out for himself. He was a politician in the best tradition of local politics, who fought for the interests of the entire city but especially for the less privileged. He held a vision of how the city should be developed for the interests of the whole of the population whether in Benwell, Scotswood, Walker, Cowgate, Sandgate, Blakelaw, Lemington or Throckley. He has been the outstanding political figure of his generation. When I came all those years ago to work in the government office, the North Region consisted of the five counties: Cumbria, Northumberland, Tyne and Wear, Durham and Cleveland/Teesside. Local authorities and the private sector mirrored this when they set up the Northern Development Company which was a major influence in bringing inward investment over two decades. As such, the region as a body was well respected, not least in Whitehall. Since then, it has allowed itself, in stages, to be dismembered, with a consequential serious loss of influence. Cumbria splintered off to join Lancashire; Teesside went for autonomy; Northumberland, Tyne and Wear, and Durham split in two. My major regret is that Jeremy, who understood the importance of the North East and saw Newcastle as its natural capital – and who was by far its ablest local politician – was never given the chance to maintain the integrity of the region, and to argue on its behalf. He would have done so excellently.

Alastair Balls

## Justice, justice shalt thou pursue …

I lived in Newcastle from 1983-92, teaching in local secondary schools, and was Secretary of the Tyneside and District Anti-Fascist Association and involved with the Labour Party. I knew of Jeremy as Leader of the Council of course, but I don't think we ever met. It was years later, in 2013, after I founded the national human rights education charity *Journey to Justice (JtoJ),* that we met in Newcastle. I interviewed Jeremy to hear what he thought of our idea. He spoke in a compelling and persuasive way about the need to ensure all forms of justice – social, economic and legal – and about the importance of challenging the politics of fear and division with its anti-immigrant, racist rhetoric. He quoted the biblical injunction, "Justice, justice shalt thou pursue" and said our project was, "necessary and timely. We need to make the case for justice and human rights. They should be at the centre of politics, or the consequences will be unfortunate for social cohesion and living as a community".

We created a civil rights travelling exhibition telling stories of 'ordinary' people in the US and UK who have taken action for social justice. *JtoJ* teaches about human rights movements and the arts and about non-violent, creative tactics. Our mission is to galvanise people to become activists themselves.

We worked with a fantastic range of organisations in the North East and had a wonderful launch at the Discovery Museum where our exhibition was housed in April 2015. Over 3,000 people visited and it was the catalyst for a programme of arts and education events organised by a cross-community group, co-ordinated alongside community artist

Bethany Elen Coyle. Jeremy spoke at the showing of *Brother Outsider* about the life of Dr Martin Luther King Junior's right hand man, Bayard Rustin. Dr King's visit to receive an honorary degree from Newcastle University in 1967 was one of the reasons for *JtoJ* choosing to have the launch in the North East, and took place thanks to an invitation from *JtoJ* friend Professor Brian Ward.

Jeremy has been a kind and generous supporter of *JtoJ* from the start. He made a big personal donation to the charity and co-hosted, with Lord Herman Ouseley, an event at the House of Lords for young people with whom we were working in Leyton, East London. They had a chance to share their poetry and ideas for addressing the social justice issues they cared about. Jeremy gave me a fascinating and entertaining tour of the House of Lords, pointing out pictures of the nation's *mishpocha*. When we had a chance to talk of things other than *JtoJ*, I found out a little more about his history, which is not too different from mine: he, too, belongs to a Jewish family of immigrants who came to Tyneside in the late 19th century. I am a descendant of the Callers: my mum Sonia, née Caller, was born in Elswick to Louis and Lily Caller (née Balkind). Her grandfather, Isaac Caller, established Callers and Sons Cabinetmakers after arriving from Amstibava, in what is now Belarus.

I know Jeremy has had a lifetime of dedicated service in the public sector and there will be many roles he held which I don't know about. What moved me most when he talked about his work was the pride he took in being Chair of Social Services because of the difference he could make. Change can be effected by all sorts of means. What a fantastic example Jeremy has set of the potential power of choosing to hold political office – locally and nationally – in these cynical times. Thank you, Jeremy, for all you did and do to make ours a society with more fairness at its heart.

Carrie Supple

*JtoJ has a website on which one can find project details and examples of material relating to many of the events mentioned in this essay, including the interview with Jeremy Beecham: www.journeytojustice.org.uk*

*A man of strong principle and virtue …*

In 1983, I was privileged to be offered the position of Assistant Director of Social Services with Newcastle City Council. I say "privileged" because the council had an excellent reputation as a progressive authority led by Jeremy Beecham, who was young, able and highly respected. He was held in high regard on both the local and national stage.

A decade earlier, the Local Authority Social Services Act of 1970 had established social services departments following the recommendations of the Seebohm Report in 1968. Fortunately for Newcastle, Jeremy Beecham was made Chair of Social Services in Newcastle in the 1970s, a time when integrated social services were in their infancy. He clearly understood that two of the central precepts of Seebohm were the keys to success: recognising the benefits of, and supporting, *care in the community* and *preventative care.* During his tenure at Newcastle social services he had the vision and political will to increase significantly the provision of home care services for elderly people, and for those with disabilities, to enable them to remain in their own homes. This was years ahead of the national agenda espoused in the Community Care Act 1990, that sought amongst other things to achieve similar outcomes. Furthermore, in those early years he ensured that the new department was well funded.

By the time I arrived, the council was having to address a significant reduction in resources. Jeremy, as its leader, proved to be a formidable operator in persuading political colleagues to accept these strictures. Some local authorities at the time prepared illegal deficit budgets to avoid the service cuts, but Jeremy made it quite clear, publicly, that he would never countenance the council breaking the law under his leadership. A man of strong principle and virtue.

He is a great admirer of Richard III (the historical person, not the malignant character portrayed by Shakespeare). I joked with him once that he was more like a Roman consul – say, Cicero – by nature: lawyerly, principled and a great believer in constitutional protocols. He took the point graciously, but I lost the argument!

In later years, the Theatre Royal was facing severe financial difficulties, and I became the finance director of a newly appointed management team. Having Sir Jeremy (as he became) on the board of directors made the job easier, particularly as the political situation around the Arts was vexed at the time. An ardent supporter of the Arts in the city, he argued passionately that the city needed *all* sectors of the economy to thrive. The Theatre Royal still operates today thanks to him and others giving their time, energy and wisdom.

Blessed with keen intelligence and wit, he has contributed greatly to Newcastle's reputation as an attractive, cosmopolitan city. He operated the levers of power effectively to deliver quality services, particularly to the less advantaged, during periods of severe financial constraint. Newcastle has been fortunate indeed to have had such a visionary leader who eschewed parochial obscurantism in favour of promoting all aspects of city life.

In short, a man of integrity and deep commitment to the city.

Graham Armstrong
Social Services (Asst Director and Director) 1983-1999
Theatre Royal (Director of Finance) 1999-2008

*"I like Newcastle. It is a city I can do business with."*

In 2013 the Urban Design Group, the professional organisation for urban designers, chose to hold its annual conference in Newcastle. As a relatively prominent local member I was asked to make a contribution to the conference focused on 'civic leadership and its impact on the quality of place'. This request prompted me to reflect on cities that were widely viewed to have been significantly improved over the previous 10-20 years, the involvement of civic leadership in these improvements and, from this, I tried to distil some defining characteristics of the nature of civic leadership in these places.

It was not surprising that these reflections quickly bought me to my experience of the civic leadership that Jeremy Beecham brought to my own city over the seventeen years of his leadership of the council. I appreciated this at first-hand, initially as a senior planner working on regeneration in the West End and then – for over ten years – as the council's Environmental Design Officer, heading up a wide range of design, conservation and environmental activity within the wider planning service.

My defining characteristics included:

- a deep passion for the wellbeing of the place and its residents

- an ability to resolve the inevitable conflict between investment and action with highly identifiable very local benefits which brought wider, possibly less readily tangible, benefits to the city as a whole

- establishing a sense of ambition, purpose and direction which was widely shared within and between the political parties – and factions within parties – bringing the stability necessary for the creation and delivery of longer-term policies and strategies

- a willingness to work in partnership with external agencies and with government, regardless of differences of political persuasion

- a mutually supportive culture in relationship with officers, based on shared concern and enthusiasm and mutual respect and in which officers felt empowered to explore, develop and exploit ways of progressing the aspirations for the city.

Working for the city throughout Jeremy's leadership I saw all of these characteristics in full flow through his pattern of operation.

An early example was watching him work with senior officers in the council's legal and property departments, encouraging imaginative responses to the challenges in keeping the BBC in the city by helping them relocate from very poor quality accommodation in a former maternity hospital opposite the Laing Gallery. This resulted in their eventual move to new, purpose built accommodation in the form of the 'Pink Palace' on Barrack Road.

On the political front, I worked with him on approaches to the handling of Vickers' vacation of its Elswick Works within the recently designated Enterprise Zone. Jeremy readily appreciated that this was overall a very challenging site: left to the market, the easy parts of this would be developed leaving the more substantial opportunities unexploited. He was clear that the best way forward was for the council to buy the site and to find a development partner who would work with it to secure its comprehensive development. The Labour group had a very strong majority on the council and were clearly ready to back this direction of action. Regardless of this he brought into the decision-making process the leader of the opposition Lib Dem group – and even brought in the former leader of the Conservative group, which no longer had any members of council. The all-party consensus on the action, and the behind-the-scenes conversations between local Conservatives and their national colleagues, may well have proved instrumental in securing support from the Conservative government of the day. Generosity of spirit, or simply wise political behaviour? Whatever it was, the sharing of purpose and direction which this reflected was clearly effective, with the purchase of the site and the delivery of the relatively in-town business park of the Armstrong Centre through a development partner flowing from it.

This acceptance of the political reality of the need to reach accommodations with Margaret Thatcher's Conservative government attracted a comment from Environment Minister Michael Heseltine: "I like Newcastle. It is a city I can do business with". This was in stark contrast to the position adopted by Derek Hatton in Liverpool. I have no doubt as to which of these two served their cities better, despite the inevitable criticism the Heseltine accolade must have attracted from members of Jeremy's own Labour group.

A similar pattern of engagement with the Conservative government-created Tyne and Wear Development Corporation sought effectively to secure the best outcomes possible for the parts of the city within the development area where Newcastle City Council could no longer control development, and to minimise potential impacts on the remainder of the city.

This thinking was paralleled with a positive and imaginative approach to the parts of the city centre which lay outside the areas of investment through the development corporation – a key part of which was the revival of the southern part of the city's centre through the Grainger Town Project. For me, the development of this project brought the richest picture of Jeremy's pattern of working with officers and his fellow politicians to exploit opportunities to protect and improve the part of the city which might have most suffered from its commercial life being sucked towards the development activity on the Quayside.

Even without competition from the Quayside, the historic southern part of the city centre – based around the streets developed by Grainger in the 1840s – were suffering. Years of intense working with City Grant and other funding sources had seen individual buildings rescued whilst others around them slipped into vacancy and dereliction.

With his strong interest in historic environments, doubtless triggered by pride in Newcastle's heritage, Jeremy had become an English Heritage Commissioner. Lighting on the potential of a new initiative from English Heritage in the form of 'Conservation Area Partnerships', I suggested that the council should make a play for one of the pilot schemes. My conversations with Jeremy about this proposal were clearly pushing at an open door: he supported wholeheartedly the need for the City Council to concentrate its limited conservation investment into the Grainger Town area if we were to bid successfully. Further, he managed the background politics of local disappointment in other parts of the city from which the limited funding was diverted, which was an inevitable part of the necessary focusing of investment.

The bid was successful and secured by far the largest financial allocation of the eventual thirteen partnership pilots across England. From this grew a conservation-led regeneration programme. This, in turn, grew into the major European-funding-supported and Europa Nostra Award-winning Grainger Town Project which necessarily operated with close involvement of the council – but at arm's length from it.

Without Jeremy's appreciation of the potential of the initial conservation partnership bid and his willingness to address its modest implications elsewhere in the city – and his establishing a climate of willingness in the council for working through arm's length organisations – the significant achievements of the Grainger Town Project in stabilising and improving the southern parts of the city centre which followed on from his leadership would have been lost. Shared pride in its appearance was not enough on its own!

After the leadership of Newcastle City Council passed to Tony Flynn I continued to support and work with Jeremy in his role as the chair of the development committee.

Reflecting on my relationship with Jeremy as a professional employed by the council, I realise that there was a continuum from my experience as a relatively junior officer watching from the side-lines the brokering of the relocation of the BBC and the purchase of the Vickers Elswick site, through to being a highly trusted, more senior, officer later in my career. That said, this relationship of deep trust felt exceptional for someone who was not a chief officer or even a deputy chief officer. I am sure, however, that I was far from alone in feeling that, despite my lack of formal status, I had a relationship with Jeremy that would have been very rare in other contexts and with other leaders of council.

Returning to the last of my defining characteristics for effective civic leadership … I appreciate that the trust which must underpin a mutually supportive relationship between civic leaders and officers cannot be freely given; it has to be earned. The beginning of my own journey of trust was one that revealed admirable human qualities:

As Newcastle City Council Environmental Design Officer, I was responsible for presenting the council's views on any major development they were referring to the Royal Fine Arts Commission. I had appreciated from my first couple of sessions that a one-page note with a maximum of six key points – which could be left with the RFAC for subsequent reference – was the ideal basis for a presentation to their meetings in London. Given the prominence and sensitivity of anything referred to the RFAC, the preparation process for this involved clearing the points to be covered with both the City Planning Officer and with Jeremy.

Quite early in my ten years in the post I had to handle the first attempt at proposals, through the Tyne and Wear Development Corporation, for the comprehensive redevelopment of East Quayside – extending from the Crown Courts to the mouth of the Ouseburn. In my professional view these proposals were very deeply flawed. To open up discussion at the RFAC of the council's concerns regarding these flaws, my note ran to an exceptional *twelve* key points. Jeremy called me down to his office to discuss the note. Against the background of his attempting to build a constructive relationship with the Corporation, my suggested criticisms of its flagship development were problematic: "We can't say all this!" was his opener. Together, we reviewed the issues carefully. Whilst he agreed with what I'd written, he felt that the City Council could not tactically afford to be so heavily critical of the proposals. Respecting this, I agreed to focus on only six of the twelve points and amended the briefing note accordingly.

A week after the RFAC meeting, a copy of their letter to the developers and the Tyne and Wear Development Corporation arrived at the council. I was immediately summoned by Jeremy to explain myself. "We agreed you wouldn't pursue all of the points of criticism you raised in your draft – but here they all are in the RAFC's letter!" All I could do was to hand him my agreed six-point briefing note, assuring him that I had spoken accordingly, and that the Royal Commission's members were not dumb and had picked up on the rest of the points themselves. All in all, for many people this would *not* have been a great start, but clearly, given the subsequent development of a very trusting relationship, Jeremy must have given me the benefit of the doubt on my actions as well as respect for this confirmation of my professional views.

For me a final – and hugely telling – mark of the personal quality of a man who appreciated and valued committed officers came when I left Newcastle City Council in 1999. Two days after my departure I received a letter from the (by then) back-bench Councillor Beecham thanking me personally for all that I had done in support of the city, and in support of him. It was by far the most wonderful "thank you" I could have received. The only response I could make was to thank him so much for the opportunities he had given me – I hope productively – to serve my adopted city.

Colin Haylock

*He provided leadership during difficult days …*

More than forty years ago I arrived in Newcastle upon Tyne. I had been appointed Priority Area Team Leader at Newcastle City Council, for the East City, St Lawrence and St Anthony's wards. This was my first contact with Jeremy Beecham, who was then Leader of the City Council; he had first been elected to the council in 1967, as member for Benwell, in opposition to the Conservative group that was in control.

I went on to work directly for Jeremy as his PA. Ten years later I took up the role as head of Newcastle City Challenge, the West End Partnership. Jeremy chaired the City Challenge board.

My move to Newcastle contrasted with my life in Edinburgh, working at Edinburgh University, where my time had been spent on research such as the impact of tourism in the south of England, oil development in the Highlands of Scotland, and the economy of rural communities in National Parks. I had been recruited to Newcastle City Council for my experience in community development: I had lived for about ten years in the run-down west of Edinburgh where I had helped a youth club secure funds to convert a former public washhouse into a sports centre and had also joined the movement to save tenements from demolition. Much of the area to the west of Edinburgh city centre had been zoned for redevelopment, notably the extension of the breweries that gave its West End a distinctive aroma.

In Newcastle I was to work in Byker for councillors such as Jon

Gower Davies, an academic who had published a critique of Newcastle's redevelopment policies and community organisations. Byker had been subject to this redevelopment; Newcastle's reputation as a radical planning authority was well known, and as a planning student I had visited Byker, and had seen the work of the photographer Sirkka-Liisa Konttinen, which documented the demolition of its Victorian terraced houses and the community that would disappear with them.

The Byker Wall in 1975, built to replace Victorian terraced houses.

I could also see the legacy of the T. Dan Smith era, during which a period of extensive rebuilding had taken place in both the city's centre and surrounding neighbourhoods; the results of this period of redevelopment could be seen across the city. Perhaps most significantly the construction of the Central Motorway had driven a trench through the city centre.

Jon Gower Davies had captured this movement in *The Evangelistic Bureaucrat*, published some ten years before, detailing the comprehensive redevelopment of Georgian and Victorian terraces in the Rye Hill area of Newcastle. The before and after images in his book illustrate the planning

... the Central Motorway had driven a trench through the city centre.

blight that was the result of a policy of 'cold storage' – the City Council buying up houses and leaving them empty.

Jeremy Beecham, who was elected Leader of the Council in 1977, had replaced the adversarial relationship between council and communities with a more consensual and delegated system of regeneration, aided by a modest budget for the most deprived wards, known as Priority Areas. This spirit of partnership was recognised a decade later, when Jeremy noted – in the final review of the City Challenge programme – that the "regeneration of the West End had benefited from working together in partnership".

Jeremy's leadership of the council presented a different approach from that of his predecessors to tackling the deep-seated problems in the city. The decline and disappearance of industry on the River Tyne had been replaced by employment in the service sector across the city centre and Gateshead Metrocentre. His role during his leadership of the council, and subsequently as chair of the development committee, also saw major growth beyond the Western Bypass – still going on today – a revitalised city centre serving a regional role, rehabilitation of the historic core in Grainger Town, and the transformation of the Quayside and Elswick riverside, and the creation of riverside industrial areas, such as Newburn and Walker

Together with his successors Tony Flynn and Nick Forbes, Jeremy adapted to successive government initiatives for cities and secured continued support for neighbourhood renewal, as well as strengthening the city's role in the North East of England.

This was particularly the case in the West End: the areas around North Benwell, Elswick, Arthur's Hill and Scotswood had declined significantly. He managed to keep the momentum going to enable the rebuilding of much of the Victorian city, with selective demolition and new housing, which also continues today.

Rye Hill houses in 'cold storage'. Image from J G Davies' *The Evangelistic Bureaucrat*.

That revival of Newcastle, illustrated by Jon Gower Davies' images of urban decay in Rye Hill, can be contrasted today with the flourishing Georgian terraces featured in the TV series, *A House Through Time*, presented by Professor David Olusoga.

Jeremy's great legacy to Newcastle has been his success in regenerating much of the city. His was a period of stability and continuity that for over half a century enabled parts of the city to be rebuilt and restored.

One of Jeremy's talents was his oratory. In my role as PA I had to prepare briefing notes for council meetings. These were quickly digested and then presented to the full council, in support of or against a particular motion. This ability was best demonstrated on Holocaust Memorial Day, when he produced, without notes, a searing account of the Holocaust, liberally illustrated by references to the work of Primo Levi and others.

My most difficult job working alongside Jeremy was the regeneration of the west end of Newcastle – the City Challenge programme – a five year initiative between 1991 and 1996. I was appointed having spent about three years at the Audit Commission, based in Leeds. There had been extensive television coverage of the disturbances in Meadow Well, Elswick, and Scotswood. Crime and anti-social behaviour had created conditions in which homes were abandoned, enabling investors to snap up properties for a few hundred pounds. Jeremy, as Chair of the West End Partnership, had convened a board of local residents, including the charismatic local resident Jackie Haq, business representatives such as Sue Wilson from Vickers Armstrong, and councillors for the area, including Tony Flynn. The area covered was substantial, from the Western Bypass beyond Scotswood into the centre of the city. There was a vast array of challenges: crime and antisocial behaviour, poor health, derelict housing, ageing and redundant shopping centres, long term unemployment … all features of the decline of the area.

Jeremy always encouraged very open discussion at the board meetings. Another of his talents was to make the representatives of the various sectors feel included. In practice the business sector looked to the community leaders for a lead. At the end of the first year Jeremy felt that there should be some fine tuning of the agreed budget for the £37m City Challenge government grant. The community sector felt that there should be greater support for community development and detached work with young people. Fresh projects had also emerged, such as a new health centre in Benwell.

Jeremy chaired a dramatic board meeting at which strong cases were made for modifications that would be at the expense of further demolition. The board decided to go with the changes, subject to government approval, at the first annual review, allowing a change in priorities.

At the annual review meeting Jeremy presented a clear case, facing Minister John Redwood MP. Jeremy's leadership gave credibility to the case. He was open to criticism in debate, modest in his achievements, and keen to recognise the achievements of others. This was particularly the case with the educational achievement strategy: long term investment in literacy and numeracy in the early years of education was seen as key to arresting the decline in educational standards. Minister Redwood left the meeting convinced that this was an essential intervention to secure the regeneration of the West End. He accepted the changes.

Professor Fred Robinson of Durham University, who conducted an independent evaluation of the City Challenge programme, concluded that in this period much was achieved, including reduced crime, improved physical infrastructure, and – significantly – that the regeneration would continue beyond the five years. The decline of the area was stabilised, local communities saw a marked improvement in the locality, manifested by reduced crime … although the experience of crime would leave a long term mark, one which took a long time to disappear.

Jeremy Beecham's legacy is to have stayed with the area during a period of considerable challenges, renewal and redevelopment. He provided leadership during difficult days, and was appreciative of the contribution of many people. Much of this revival can be seen in the terraces of the West End, and the transformation of the riverbank. Scotswood Road has a new life as a modern entrance to the city.

Jonathan Blackie CBE
Former Regional Director, Government Office North East (2002-11)
Director of Newcastle City Challenge (1992-96)
Professional Assistant to the Leader of Newcastle City Council (1984-87)

## Jeremy Beecham: Our Northern Star

In the summer of 1967, the Beatles released their iconic album *Sgt Pepper's Lonely Hearts Club Band,* that was lauded by *The Times* critic Kenneth Tynam as "a decisive moment in the history of Western Civilisation". A month earlier on 1 May 1967, a young 22-year-old Jeremy Beecham was elected as a councillor for Benwell, one of the poorest areas in Newcastle's West End, without any such fanfare. Jeremy represented this ward for 55 years until he retired this year due to ill health. Nevertheless, for many years Jeremy received national acclaim as the foremost local government spokesperson in the country.

At the age of 16, Jeremy joined the Young Socialists, where he cut his political teeth and met his future wife, Brenda, who became the mother of their two children Richard and Sara – their pride and joy. He attended the Royal Grammar School in Newcastle where he was reportedly the brightest boy in his class. He graduated from the University of Oxford with a first-class degree in law. At Oxford, he became Secretary of the Labour Club which set him on a path towards political life. When he returned to Newcastle, he started work as a solicitor and eventually became a partner in the firm Henderson, Beecham and Peacock.

When Labour returned to power in Newcastle in 1974, Jeremy became Chair of Social Services. As a lifelong advocate of public services, he doubled the number of home help workers and 'meals on wheels' deliveries on his first day in office. Jeremy later described this as his finest hour in politics.

In 1977, Jeremy was elected Leader of the City Council, a position he held for seventeen years – making him the longest serving leader in Newcastle's history. During his tenure of office, he rose to national prominence becoming the chair of the Association of Metropolitan Authorities (later retitled the Local Government Association). He was awarded a knighthood for his service to local government. Jeremy was also recognised within the city, gaining an honorary doctorate from Newcastle University and becoming an Honorary Freeman of Newcastle. He was proud to become the chair of the Labour Party's National Executive Committee leading him to chair the Labour Party Conference.

Freeman of the City

When Jeremy stood down as Leader of the Council in 1994, he was elevated to the House of Lords becoming Baron Beecham of Benwell serving as Shadow Minister for Health and Social Services. Unusually, he continued to serve as a councillor for Benwell during this period – keeping in touch with the needs of the public. He also believed that this gave some democratic legitimacy to his role in the House of Lords.

Unfortunately, for all but two of the years that he was Leader of the Council, the Tories were in power nationally. Margaret Thatcher (Prime Minister from 1979 to 1990) was determined to reduce the power of local government, forcing cuts in public services and favouring privatisation. This put local politicians on the back foot, forcing them to defend public services where possible – as Neil Kinnock, the Labour Leader of the Opposition, put it, "carrying a dented shield". Consequently, Jeremy had less freedom to implement radical change than had his Labour predecessor T. Dan Smith. However, he made a significant impact on the redevelopment of Newcastle City Centre and to the welfare of the people of the city.

Jeremy's leadership was highly respected across the political spectrum, both locally and nationally, because of his outstanding intellect, pragmatism, forensic attention to detail and playful wit.

Jeremy had been fiercely proud of his record as Chair of Social Services. However, in a dark twist of fate, as Leader of the Council he had to oversee the closure of 40 residential homes for the elderly and 30 children's homes because of Margaret Thatcher's programme of privatisation. All public provision of social care is now contracted to the private sector. The resulting crisis in social care was exposed during the recent Covid-19 pandemic.

When Jeremy was the chair of the Local Government Association, he confronted the Tory government about the inequalities of local-government funding, where higher grants were given to the richer South East Councils. Sadly his arguments were cavalierly dismissed by the government.

Unlike the Tory government, Jeremy supported decentralisation and devolution. He instigated a bottom-up system of 'Priority Area Teams' allocating funds to councillors in the poorest areas of the city so that they could engage with their local communities through public meetings to determine the priorities for local spending.

Nationally, Jeremy was perceived as a centralist because of his response to the implementation of the controversial Poll Tax. Some Labour councils, such as Liverpool, directly challenged the government by not setting a rate. As a solicitor, Jeremy's view was that since the Labour Party aspired to be law makers in government they should not be law breakers in opposition, even though he strongly opposed the introduction of the Poll Tax as the chair of the Local Government Association.

Drab and coal-darkened: Newcastle Quayside before renovation.

While disagreeing with many of the Conservative government's policies, Jeremy was prepared to work with it if he saw benefits to local people. As a result, Newcastle significantly profitted from an injection of money and regeneration through schemes like City Challenge that invested in the West End and the Urban Development Corporation that rejuvenated the Quayside. Jeremy was greatly admired locally as a person of intelligence and integrity who had the city's best interest at heart and was a "safe pair of hands".

The iconic Theatre Royal, bought by the council in 1971 to save it from closing. Jeremy ensured that it had the resources to find its former glory.

Before he gained political power, Jeremy had ambitions to become a Member of Parliament and stood for Labour in Tynemouth, which was a safe Tory seat at the time, against the veteran MP Dame Irene Ward. Later he attempted to gain the nomination for MP for Newcastle East but the local Labour Constituency Party selected Mike Thomas instead, believing he was the more left-wing candidate. Thomas later defected to the newly formed Social Democratic Party. Personally, I am sure Jeremy was Cabinet material. However, because Labour was in opposition nationally for eighteen years, in hindsight Jeremy was probably happy that he spent his political career in power locally rather than in opposition nationally.

Jeremy was easily a match for any government minister. Many remember with amusement his introduction of Michael Howard at a Local Government Association's Annual General Meeting. Jeremy recalled that many Cambridge alumni have had notable careers such as John Gummer, Norman Lamont and Michael Howard in the 1960s and Donald Maclean, Guy Burgess and Kim Philby in the 1930s. "I will leave it up to you to decide who did the most damage to this country." Jeremy sat down to hoots of laughter, leaving Howard lost for words, for comparing Tory ministers with Soviet spies.

Jeremy had a 'hinterland'. He was an avid reader of literature, attended concerts of classical music and enjoyed theatre, supporting the Theatre Royal politically and personally. He had a season ticket to St James' Park, the home of Newcastle United, where he had ample opportunity to voice his frustration at their many poor performances. Although he valued privacy in his personal life, Jeremy had a devoted group of friends and threw a good party with his wife Brenda, who sadly passed away in 2010.

I was Jeremy's deputy for five years before I succeeded him as Leader of the Council. He was both a friend and a mentor whose contribution to the city and local government nationally is unrivalled. He was an outstanding Leader of the Council and the foremost national advocate for local government. Jeremy was our Northern Star, shining in the firmament, giving us clear-sighted direction. Many lesser politicians' star status rose and fell and their light slowly dimmed, but not Jeremy's. Jeremy was loyal, public-spirited, and devoted to the people of Newcastle. The brightest star in the sky: our Northern Star.

Tony Flynn
Deputy Leader of the Council to Jeremy Beecham for five years and then succeeded him as Leader 1994 to 2004

*Beecham was, I believe, a sincere fighter*
*for the interests of the most deprived …*

Looking back 50 years from 2021 to 1971, when I moved to Newcastle to work as a reporter on the *Evening Chronicle*, and speaking as one of the millions of pedestrians who walk through and busy themselves in the brick and stone stories of the city in which I live, as the introduction to this book puts it, the face of the city, if not unrecognisable, was then certainly very different from today.

Much of the Georgian Eldon Square had already been demolished, leaving only the east terrace, but the new shopping centre destined for the site had not yet been built and it was in use as a car park where I would sometimes leave my Mini when bringing the family into town for Saturday shopping in the Grainger Market. The old Cattle Market, where Times Square and the Centre for Life now stand, was another site I would use for parking.

In another personal reminiscence, after we moved to Jesmond not long afterwards my walk to work would take me through Brandling Park, where the trees were painted white with the acronym SOCEM – name and slogan of the anti-motorway campaign group Save Our City from Environmental Mess. When I arrived daily at my desk in Thomson House in the Groat Market, I looked out over the Victorian Old Town Hall as it was, demolished in 1973 and replaced by the pub and office building we see there today.

And if today I do not want to walk, I can take the Metro into the city centre – a convenience which was still almost a decade away for Tyneside and three decades off for my native Wearside.

My occasional visits to watch Newcastle United – only occasional because as a Mackem I am of course a Sunderland supporter – would see me standing in the East Stand Paddock of what was then a completely un-redeveloped St James' Park. Nearby stood the Scottish & Newcastle Brewery, now site of the Helix science and business park, and in Strawberry Place the now demolished New St James' Hall, where I once watched the great Masambula and other stars of the wrestling ring.

You may ask what any of this has to do with Jeremy Beecham. And the answer, surprisingly, is very little, at least directly. Because, for all the changes that have taken place to the fabric of Newcastle during his 50-plus years as a city councillor, including 17 years as leader, he had little personal involvement in the physical redevelopment of the city. But that does not mean he did not play an important, indirect, enabling role, as we will see.

As I was settling into my work in the newsroom of the *Evening Chronicle*, Beecham was in the early stages of a political career that would take him to the leadership of Newcastle City Council for 17 years, to the chair of the Local Government Association, the chair of the Labour Party's national executive committee and eventually a seat in the House of Lords. If, on the way, he had little direct involvement in the physical redevelopment of Newcastle, it was partly a matter of deliberate choice, as we shall see. What he did do, however, was to ensure as far as possible a stable political environment in which the grand designs of others could be pursued. That was no mean feat, given the legacy of corruption which had tainted the politics of the North East in the era of T. Dan Smith, jailed for six years in 1974 for corruption, and Andrew Cunningham, another powerful North East Labour politician jailed for corruption in 1974, in his case for five years, reduced on appeal to three.

Beecham also ensured as far as possible a stable financial environment for the council, which was no less a challenge in the period of what we would now call *austerity* that was about to fall on local government, as we will also see.

In late 1994, Geoff Laws, cartoonist in the Newcastle Journal and Chronicle, depicted Jeremy Beecham as a medieval knight.

There were three reasons for Beecham's relative lack of involvement in the physical redevelopment of Newcastle, given his leading position for so long:

One was that many of the grand designs that have so transformed Newcastle over the past 50 years either pre-dated Beecham's period as leader and even as a councillor, at least in the planning, or post-dated his leadership if not his membership of the council; he retained his old seat for the deprived ward of Benwell in the city's West End, even after taking his new one in the House of Lords as Baron Beecham of Benwell and Newcastle-upon-Tyne in 2010.

He was still at University College Oxford, where he gained a first-class degree in law, when Dan Smith was drawing up and starting to implement his modernist plans for Newcastle – all tower blocks, offices, motorways and raised walkways to separate vehicles from pedestrians and even a scheme to deck over the Tyne between Newcastle and Gateshead. Smith had discovered architectural modernism just as the Europeans who had pioneered it between the two world wars, under the likes of Le Corbusier, Gropius and the Bauhaus, were going off the idea.

To the extent that Smith's plans were carried through at all, the job was done by his immediate Conservative successors. The Tories under Arthur Grey won control of Newcastle in 1967, the year the 22-year-old Beecham was first elected to the council. Grey was not a councillor elected for four years by the people but an alderman, elected for six years by the councillors – a title and a procedure reminding us today of what a different period that was, as does of course the very thought of the Tories controlling Newcastle, where no Conservative has won a seat on the council since 1992.

Grey stood down from the leadership in 1972, shortly before I became municipal reporter of the *Chronicle*, and was succeeded by Alderman John Cox, another Tory. Grey resigned the leadership not because he was forced out, or through fatigue, or a modest belief that someone else should have a chance. Far from it. The effusive and irrepressible Grey, a Dickensian figure with his moustache and his thumbs stuck in the waistcoat of his expensive, tailored tweed suits, gave up the leadership out of his vanity. He wanted to be, and was, Lord Mayor before the opportunity was lost.

The position of Lord Mayor of Newcastle was and still is, as far as I know, awarded according to the principle of 'Buggins' turn': it went each year to the longest-serving council member of the majority party who had never held the position before, provided that person was willing to accept a post which is purely ceremonial. Its duties, at least in those days, were to chair the monthly council meetings, act as a sort of ambassador for the city, attending or presiding at formal occasions and hosting VIP visitors. Its perks were the honour and prestige, the scarlet robe that was worn and the mace that was carried ahead on ceremonial occasions, the posh car, the pair of ornate lamp posts which for some reason I never discovered were erected outside the Lord Mayor's private home, and access to the official hospitality drinks cabinet which I was once told by someone in a position to know was an opportunity of which no Lord Mayor ever failed to take advantage.

Beecham, in spite of his 50 years and more on the council, has never been Lord Mayor of Newcastle. He preferred the reality of power which he would have had to give up to the ephemeral advantages and empty vanities of a ceremonial post. Grey, however, believed that he could be Lord Mayor and still – through force of personality, honed as Dan Smith's old sparring partner – wield influence as powerful as the holding of any committee chair or other leadership position.

What is more, Grey wanted to make history by being the only person in recent times to be Lord Mayor two years running. The 'Buggins' turn' principle normally meant that once one had served one's year one stood down and made way for the next in line. But not Grey. He also wanted to make history by being the last person to be Lord Mayor of the old Newcastle, which was about to be expanded geographically but weakened administratively in the local government reforms introduced by Ted Heath's Conservative government. Geographically, Newcastle gained the urban districts of Gosforth and Newburn and the rural district of Castle Ward, but administratively it became a lower-tier local authority to the new metropolitan county council of Tyne and Wear, losing in the process its power over such important functions as transport, planning and economic development as well as less politically charged responsibilities such as museums and galleries and less glamorous ones like waste disposal. Grey, I heard at the time though could never gather the evidence to stand up a news story, had a battle at the time with Viscount Ridley, then the Conservative chair of Northumberland County Council, over who would get the small, up-market, Tory-voting commuter town of Ponteland when the local government boundaries were re-drawn. Ridley won, and Ponteland stayed in the county, giving the Tories a fighting chance of retaining control, though in fact Northumberland remained in Labour hands until 2017. Grey's fear that the new boundaries would leave the Conservatives fatally wounded in Newcastle unless Ponteland was handed to the city, proved well founded. It remained in Labour hands for 30 years, and even then it was the Liberal Democrats, not the Conservatives, who took over.

Grey could see the writing on the wall and chose to leave the council altogether in 1974 and to join instead the new Tyne and Wear Metropolitan County Council, where he was immediately elected as leader of the minority – but not at the time negligible – Conservative group.

Grey's departure from city politics in favour of its metropolitan counterpart deprived council chamber onlookers of the clashes that might have occurred between him and Beecham when the latter became leader of the Labour group and therefore of the council in 1977. Their very different styles would undoubtedly have made for entertaining debates – Grey brash and ebullient, Beecham forensic, but both sophisticated and witty rhetoricians.

The second reason Beecham was not closely involved in the large building projects that transformed the face of Newcastle was that following local government reorganisation in 1974 Newcastle City Council was no longer responsible for most of such developments. That responsibility passed to Tyne and Wear Metropolitan County Council and others, such as the Passenger Transport Authority and Passenger Transport Executive (now Nexus), which built the Metro light rail system.

Later came the Tyne and Wear Urban Development Corporation, established by Margaret Thatcher in 1987. That was the year she declared on the night of her third general election victory in June, "We must do something about those inner cities", and in September took her famous 'walk in the wilderness' near what was indeed known as the Wilderness Road in one of the most derelict areas of de-industrialising Teesside, which also got a development corporation that year. Two years earlier she had come to Wallsend and in response to a television reporter's question about unemployment, then at a staggering 20% in the region, urged an unspecified target audience (journalists, the unemployed, opposition politicians, the regional population as a whole?) to stop being "moaning minnies".

Tyne and Wear Development Corporation transformed Newcastle Quayside, as well as the St Peter's Riverside in Sunderland and Royal Quays in North Tyneside, during its 11-year lifetime. Newcastle Quayside was the undoubted jewel in its crown, seeing the demolition of a long, forbidding line of dank, dismal and derelict sheds to make way for high-class offices, up-market apartments, stylish hotels, gourmet restaurants and trendy bars. The redeveloped East Quayside, along with the conserved, historic riverside to its immediate west, and later Gateshead's redeveloped Baltic Quays just across the Tyne – with major cultural facilities in the Sage concert hall, home of the Royal Northern Sinfonia, and the Baltic Centre for Contemporary Art – turned the riverside into the North East's prime nightlife focus, a national and international tourist attraction and a huge boost to the city's economy.

Not everyone was happy, though. Nick Brown, Labour MP for Newcastle East, if I remember correctly, rued the lack of what we now call affordable housing, and Fred Robinson, an academic at Durham

University, contrasted the image of a modern, prosperous, fashionable Newcastle which the Quayside epitomised with the multiple deprivations that existed, and still exist, just a mile away in Byker.

The Quayside redevelopment elicited the only occasion I can remember on which Beecham expressed an architectural opinion. He mused that an Italianate campanile would look good there. Nothing came of the idea, as the council had little or no involvement in the redevelopment and Beecham lacked the enthusiasm and commitment to pursue it with any determination.

Later, when Gateshead Council decided to mark the millennium by throwing a footbridge over the Tyne to link the art gallery and concert hall of Baltic Quays with the busy nightlife of Newcastle Quayside, an episode occurred which typifies the petty rivalry and parochialism of North East politics, then and now. Gateshead, proud of its independence and resentful of the perceived arrogance of its northern neighbour and its posturing as regional capital, as well as opposed to a Tory government initiative, had refused to participate in the work of the Tyne and Wear Urban Development Corporation. Now, when Gateshead wanted to bridge the river, Newcastle refused to co-operate and denied landing rights for the structure on its shore. The dispute was eventually settled and the bridge is now a familiar and admired addition to the Tyne riverscape. But it is known to this day as the Gateshead Millennium Bridge, making clear which of the two councils is to be given the credit for it.

Newcastle later rubbed salt in the wound it had inflicted on Gateshead when it had refused to-cooperate in its plans for the bridge by using the structure's opening-eye image in a place-marketing campaign. Gateshead sent an observer to the public launch of this campaign, and someone who witnessed the report back to civic leaders told me many years afterwards: "It was as if they had brought news of the death of the king into the room".

Not that everyone on Newcastle City Council either was happy about the Urban Development Corporation's involvement in the redevelopment of the Quayside, much less the private sector interests that became important players. The chairman of the land and property committee, Councillor Margaret Collins, an old-school socialist, regarded the Quayside, and much else besides, as 'our land' or 'the city's land', and certainly did not want rights to it to be sold off. But this was a battle that Beecham could avoid and was happy to do so, for reasons we are about to come to. Urban development corporations were statutory bodies, supported by the government, and there was nothing the council could do about it apart, presumably, from following Gateshead and refusing to co-operate at all.

This brings us to Beecham's third reason for having little involvement in the physical redevelopment of the city. His main interest as a politician was not in grand building schemes but in public services, particularly social services.

Benwell, the ward he represented then and did for 54 years, is one of the most deprived in Newcastle. He took the view that while ambitious projects like the Central Motorway and the Metro light railway – which did not and do not go anywhere near Benwell – might be necessary to ease the city's transport congestion, and while hotels, restaurants, bars, flats (sorry, apartments) and cultural facilities might be necessary to boost the city's economy and attract investors, it was social and health services, schools and social and affordable housing that were the priorities for his constituents.

The first professional involvement I had with any of the major developments in Newcastle of the past 50 years was on 13 January 1972, when I reported in the *Chronicle* on the approval given by the council's town planning and civic services committee for the ten-year rebuilding of St James' Park, home of Newcastle United. The work, I reported, would cost £1m over that period – a paltry amount by today's standards and vivid illustration of the effects of rocketing inflation. It was Arthur Grey who was pictured in the *Chronicle* with the Newcastle United chairman, Lord Westwood, and architect Henry Faulkner Brown with an illustration of the new East Stand. Beecham at the time was still a young opposition councillor, and if he played any part in the council's decision it was not one noticed by me.

Nor did he, as far as I could tell, play much part in the political, administrative and bureaucratic events the same year which might be thought to have been more up his street – the preparations for creating Tyne and Wear Metropolitan Council from the five existing councils, including Newcastle. The lead role on behalf of the Newcastle Labour group, then in opposition, was taken by its deputy leader, Councillor Walter Wilson. Beecham was, however, already climbing the political ladder, having been voted in as secretary of the Labour group on the council as early as 1969 and selected as Labour parliamentary candidate for Tynemouth in the 1970 general election – a seat which he failed to gain from the defending Conservative, Dame Irene Ward.

On 8 September 1972, two Newcastle councillors published a report which threw doubt on ambitious plans for both more urban motorways and the Metro, both soon to become the responsibility of Tyne and Wear County Council. The two were Councillors Norman Stockdale and Ken Skethaway. Once again Beecham was not involved. Newcastle's urban motorway network was eventually restricted to the one road we see today, running north from the Tyne Bridge; plans for a Central Motorway West slicing from what are now the Redheugh Bridge and St James' Boulevard through the Leazes area to the Haymarket never went ahead, while the only evidence that remains of plans for a Central Motorway East bypass is to be seen in a few metres of planned junction in Shieldfield, now going nowhere.

However, three months later the government did approve plans for the Metro and awarded a grant of £49m to cover 75% of the cost. The news came in a letter from Transport Minister John Peyton to the chairman of the Tyne and Wear Passenger Transport Authority (PTA), Alderman Andrew Cunningham, three months after a rather embarrassing visit by Peyton to Newcastle. He met members of the PTA at the Royal Station

Hotel but declined to be photographed with Cunningham, whose 1974 trial for his role in the Poulson scandal – which also destroyed the career of Dan Smith – was then widely anticipated.

While Beecham may not have been involved in these high-profile shenanigans over grand projects, he was not idle. His activity, however, was directed at an issue of potentially greater immediate concern to his constituents in Benwell: council house rents. In 1972 the government introduced a Housing Finance Bill under which rents were to rise by £1 from October 1. Any councils that did not implement the rise would see their homes taken over by civil servants who would act as commissioners responsible to the secretary of state. Two North East councils – Wallsend and South Shields – decided to defy the government. Beecham and other Labour members attacked the so-called 'Fair Rents Bill' at the council meeting in September 1972, but there is no record, and I have no memory, that they threatened to refuse to implement the Act. How the affair ended for either Wallsend, South Shields or Newcastle is now forgotten history for all but a few. It does, however, show the type of issue Beecham was concerned with as well as his general approach of protesting against government actions but remaining within the law.

The impression that Beecham gave as a young councillor, and which is preserved in my memory to this day, is thus of a politician more interested in public services for the people of his deprived ward than in grand plans of the type championed by Dan Smith and Arthur Grey. It is an impression confirmed from his own mouth in a long-forgotten interview he gave me in 1973, not long after Labour had won elections for the reconstituted council that was to take control of the expanded city the following year, at the same time as the metropolitan county council came into existence. It was by then known that Beecham would chair the social services committee.

Nineteen seventy-three was a pivotal year in the recent history of Newcastle, its elections for the new, expanded council that was to take control the following year of not just the city as it then was, but the suburbs of Gosforth, Newburn and Castle Ward. At the same time strategic responsibilities like transport and planning were to be handed over to the new Tyne and Wear Metropolitan County Council, as mentioned above. After a period of Conservative control under Arthur Grey, the council would return in 1974 to Labour for what turned out to be an extended period.

This was a time of intense debate over the future redevelopment of the city. The period between December 1972 and April 1974 saw major reports and features which I wrote about in the *Evening Chronicle* with headlines including: 'Tyne rapid transit gets £49m go-ahead'. 'Do we need this urban motorway?' 'Byker: Was it a good idea at the time?' (a reference to housing redevelopment, including the famous Byker Wall), 'Problems of planning a city', 'City redevelopment: Is it time the planners took stock' and 'Secret planning report questions City motorways'.

On 4 March 1976, Eldon Square shopping centre, site of my former car park, opened at last. On the same day that I reported on the ceremony, attended by the Lord Mayor – in full finery – and other dignitaries, I also covered a survey showing that 20% of Newcastle households were living at or below the poverty line. This conjunction of events made a persuasive emotive case for Beecham's focus on services for the deprived rather than grand schemes, though reason tells us that shopping centres are needed too, though not necessarily the one that had required the demolition of so much of Georgian Newcastle to make way for it. The opening of Eldon Square came when Beecham was still a year away from assuming the leadership of the council.

While Beecham was largely absent from these debates about development, he was working on grand plans of his own of a different kind. With Labour having won the 1973 elections and about to take over the council in 1974, and Beecham and I both aware by this time that he was to be the chairman of the social services committee, he was one of two young Labour councillors destined for senior positions who I identified as worth interviewing at length; the other was Derek Webster, who was to chair the education committee. The interview with Beecham is still worth quoting at length, for it accurately describes the course of his career for decades to come, focusing on welfare, health, social services and housing. He told me:

> *"The sort of ward I represent has a lot of this type of poverty. Now that I am to be chairman of the social services committee I want to see this type of council activity accorded a higher priority. I want to see the council ascertaining the welfare needs of people in the area, seeking out the people who need help but are not coming forward to ask for it.*
>
> *I also want to see the council doing more to look after the old and the sick in their own homes for as long as possible, and that will mean increasing our domiciliary staff – people like home helps. For those who must be taken into residential care because they cannot be properly looked after, I would like to see smaller residential units so they are more like homes and less like institutions. It will mean spending more money, but I do not believe that people will object to paying more rates [council tax] if they are told the money is for the old and the sick."*

As I wrote at the time: "Councillor Beecham's record shows that he is not a man who is afraid of controversy, yet he has not been to the fore in recent rows in the city over planning, office blocks and motorways". His interview continued:

> *"I am not basically a planning man, and perhaps I have not taken as much interest in the motorway debate as I might have done. It is not an issue that affects my ward directly. Also, I have never joined the planning committee for what I consider to be the good reason that professionally I might represent clients with an interest in planning."*

That interview, as well as confirming impressions of Beecham already discussed – his interest in public services rather than big developments, and his willingness to tax and spend as much as possible on those services – introduces one other feature that was to characterise his period as council leader: his determination to avoid the type of corruption and scandal that had marred the career of his predecessor, Dan Smith.

That interview, looking back on it nearly 50 years later, was one with which I believe both Beecham I can be pleased: Beecham because he set out with frank honesty the priorities that were to guide his entire career and the fact that he was willing to raise council tax to pursue them, and I because he was one of two young councillors who I correctly identified and chose to interview at the time as 'two young men going places in politics'. The other, Derek Webster, though he did not rise to the same heights as Beecham, spent a distinguished period as the chairman of Newcastle's education committee.

Sceptics might have thought in 1973, and might still think today, that the local government reorganisation which was supposed to increase efficiency and which was the occasion among other things of Beecham's rise to the chair of Newcastle social services committee, would in fact lead instead to a boom in town hall jobs. And that is indeed what I noticed at the time. Reorganisation, I reported in the *Chronicle* barely a month after my Beecham interview, was turning into a bonanza, with more officials, fancier titles and bigger salaries. In Newcastle, for example, five council departments were between them to have 11 more officials of the rank of assistant director or above, including social services, which would have one extra.

It was also a year which showed ominous signs of things to come for Newcastle's budget. The council, I reported, might have to cut some services, including social services, because of a government clamp down. Rates were raised by what now seems like an unthinkable 15% though this was the high-inflation era of the 1970s. Nevertheless, Newcastle, caught between high council spending and low government grants, stood out as a high-rates authority, while many other councils in the North East raised rates hardly at all. In December 1973, with Labour about to take over both Newcastle and Northumberland, the *Chronicle* reported that the government had ordered both to slash their budgets.

That was under a Conservative government. But barely had Labour taken control of the city council when another financial crisis brought another government clamp-down on spending, threatening the ambitious plans of Beecham and others. This time it was a Labour Environment Secretary, Tony Crosland, who told councils in 1975: "For the next few years times will not be normal. …[T]he party is over". Crosland meant what he said. In 1975, I reported that: "Town halls in the North East were today reeling after news of yet another crippling blow to council spending".

In 1976, I reported: "North East council leaders return this week from a meeting with Environment Secretary Mr Peter Shore [Labour] to face the prospect of having to make more cuts in their spending plans". In response to an ultimatum from Chancellor Denis Healey – Labour again – to reduce the council's budget by £7m, councillors refused to axe jobs or cut service but did agree to look for 'efficiency savings'. Only two months later I reported that North East councils were being forced to cut another £13m from their budgets. Ever since then, it seems, under governments of both parties, 'normal' has meant 'constrained' as far as council spending is concerned.

At the same time as the government was putting pressure on council budgets, Beecham was nonetheless stepping up the plans to tackle inner-city deprivation which he had outlined in his 1973 interview. Special teams of councillors and officials were set up to deal with social problems in ten of Newcastle's most disadvantaged wards and part of an eleventh, and the funding available for them was significantly increased. He even got a grant out of the government to study whether this 'priority area teams' approach could be used elsewhere. About the same time Beecham also launched a campaign to encourage more eligible children to take advantage of free school meals.

Whether Beecham created or inherited an expansionist tax-and-spend culture at Newcastle Civic Centre from his immediate Labour predecessor as council leader, Councillor Tom Collins, is hard to say at this distance in time. My memory is that it was a culture endemic to virtually all Labour councillors at the time and would have been pursued whoever was Leader of the Council; the only question was over tactics – how confrontational to be with the government. But expansion was certainly going on, in spite of the government's attempts to put downward pressure on budgets. In March 1978, a year after Beecham had become leader, I revealed a secret report by the council's chief executive warning that Newcastle's 18,000-plus workforce was growing at an unprecedented rate at a time when other councils were cutting staff.

While Beecham and other Labour councillors undoubtedly believed the big spending to be in a good cause, there was also evidence of waste and lack of financial control, exposed by two reports in the *Chronicle*. In 1979 I revealed a confidential document saying that the bonus schemes of hundreds of council workers were out of control and no one knew how much had been paid out in the past few years. When I asked Beecham if the sum could be millions he replied that he could not speculate. In 1980 I revealed a survey showing the Civic Centre typing pool to be 70% overstaffed, with 86 typists doing the work of 51.

The issue of Civic Centre staffing levels was one of a number of controversies in which Beecham, as Leader of the Council, might have been expected to play a high-profile role. But as headlines were written over subjects like the fate of the council's direct labour organisation, the mismanagement of council houses and even a strike by social workers, in which he might have been expected to take a close personal interest even though he had by then relinquished the chair of the social services committee, Beecham kept a low profile. Critics might say he was keeping his head down, supporters that he was good at delegating.

Beecham's low-key approach came to the fore in 1979, the UK's 'winter of discontent', when trade unions in both the public and private sectors (including the National Union of Journalists, of which I was a member) staged a long series of pay strikes as the government struggled to contain raging inflation. When national pay talks with town hall workers broke down, Newcastle, like other councils, faced a crisis. Beecham's response was to state that he wanted to avoid 'headlong confrontation' with the unions. Instead he would seek more exemptions from industrial action in the schools, while rubbish dumps would only be set up if it became necessary.

At the start of 1980, now under a Tory government again, this time under Margaret Thatcher, I reported that the council's budget would have to be slashed by £29m to meet government guidelines and rates might rise by 33%. There was a financial pincer movement on Newcastle's budget and ratepayers: rising inflation and the Labour council's expansionist plans for public services on one hand, and on the other the downward pressure on spending now coming from Michael Heseltine presiding at the Department of the Environment and continuing the policies seen under Labour's Tony Crosland, Peter Shore and Denis Healey. Meanwhile, trade unions representing the Civic Centre workers, who by now numbered 19,000, were threatening action against proposals to save cash including a review of bonus schemes and even redundancies.

In the midst of this turmoil Newcastle's rates rose by a whopping 34% in 1980, and by this time the city had the highest rates in England. It was singled out by Heseltine as one of the country's worst over-spenders. If the council and the government got involved in all-out war over spending cuts, as was looking more and more likely, I wrote in the *Chronicle*, it was hard to see how the council could win. Beecham travelled to London to find out just what Heseltine was planning and was shocked at what he heard. On his return he tried to placate the unions. He denied that the council was planning to 'get tough' and said it wanted co-operation, and in the end the council juggled the complex rules of local government finance to keep within government demands while avoiding swingeing cuts, and the crisis blew over. It was a typical Beecham manoeuvre.

But government pressure was relentless. Hardly had one budget crisis been dealt with than Heseltine slashed £12m from the grants that councils in Northumberland, Tyne and Wear and County Durham were expecting in 1981/82, with Newcastle the biggest loser with a reduction of £4.5m. Beecham's response at that stage was again characteristically measured, saying the council would have to look seriously at a list of cuts. In January 1981 he announced a 25% rates rise (later reduced to 22.5%) as well as £2.50 a week on council house rents, and 250 job losses.

The struggle over budgets continued in 1982. A report from the Chartered Institute of Public Finance and Accountancy revealed that not just Newcastle but councils all over the North East were among the nation's biggest spenders. Newcastle was heading for a £15m overspend the following year and Heseltine was threatening a heavy fine in response. Yet in the event, three years later, as the battle between local authorities and the Thatcher government raged on in similar vein, it was Derek Hatton, the deputy leader of Liverpool City Council, not anyone from Newcastle, who was famously denounced by Labour Party leader Neil Kinnock in 1985 for 'hiring taxis to scuttle round a city handing out redundancy notices to its own workers'. This was a reference to Liverpool's dire economic situation after its political leaders decided to play hardball with Thatcher's government and resist centrally imposed cuts, as the Liverpool Echo put it. And it was Ted Knight in Lambeth, not Beecham in Newcastle, who was surcharged £125,000 by the district auditor for refusing to set a legal budget – a move hardly imaginable from Newcastle's careful, law-abiding solicitor.

Yet, as noted above in relation to bonuses out of control and an over-staffed typing pool, there were savings that could have been be made. There was spending which was either well-intentioned but inefficient, or trivial but of a sort likely to infuriate the public. In the first category I reported that the council had been pouring so much cash into youth and community facilities in Byker that some were under-used and competing with each other to attract people. Much of the money had come from the priority area teams set up by Beecham five years earlier to channel money into deprived inner-city wards. Byker had three such wards, each spending money in its own area without having regard to what its neighbours were doing.

Into the second 'trivial but annoying' category fell the contentious issue of official hospitality. Two recent functions had cost more than £2,000 each: the Lord's Mayor's annual banquet and a visit by the Queen. The cost of the banquet included meals, drinks, cigarettes and cigars for 300 guests (of whom I might have been one). The Queen's visit cost about the same, including luncheon at the Mansion House for 34 (of whom I am sure I was not one). A significant fact about these events and their cost was that councillors discussed them in private, and I had to rely on a leak for the information.

Also at that time of financial crisis and threatened cuts, councillors were debating whether public transport was too dangerous for the elderly among them, so they should be provided with taxis after evening duties extending beyond 9.45pm rather than having to brave possible contact with drunks and rowdies on the buses, as I put it at the time. The general purposes sub-committee could not make up its mind and the eventual outcome, I'm afraid, is now probably lost in the archives.

All the while, too, on a much larger scale, controversies raged over the major developments in the hands of Tyne and Wear County Council, with the construction of tunnels and underground stations tearing the city centre apart as the Metro staggered from financial crisis to crisis, and the threat of more motorways and other large-scale road schemes divided opinion across the city.

The Metro did, however, reach an important landmark in that troubled year of 1980 when the first stage opened between Tynemouth and Haymarket. It had taken six years, required two Acts of Parliament and the agreement of six ministers of transport. It had also seen numerous crises and the expenditure of £278m since Transport Minister John Peyton had come to Newcastle to approve the original £49m grant which would supposedly meet 75% of the cost. One intervening transport minister,

I was told later, visiting Newcastle during one of the financial crises threatening the Metro, was entertained by leading councillors at a city night club to keep him sweet. If true, it worked. I am sure this was not a tactic Beecham would have used, whatever the good cause at stake.

The following year the Queen came to Tyneside to open the Metro section crossing the river from Haymarket to Heworth.

One important building development in Newcastle that did take place under the auspices of Newcastle City Council in Beecham's time was an extension of Eldon Square shopping centre. Newcastle rather than Tyne and Wear County was involved if for no other reason than that much of the land was owned by the City Council. But Beecham, true to his word, seems to have played little part in decisions about the development, perhaps for fear of a conflict of interests between his public responsibilities as council leader and professional clients as a lawyer.

Also at the time Labour in Newcastle, and Beecham personally, were facing a double-pronged political attack from both right and left. On the right, the MP for Newcastle East, Mike Thomas, had joined the new Social Democratic Party, which seemed for a time to pose a serious threat. But in the general election he would only come third, losing his seat to Newcastle councillor Nick Brown, who went on to have a long career in Labour governments, serving as chief whip under Tony Blair, Gordon Brown, Jeremy Corbyn and Keir Starmer. The SDP never posed a serious threat to Labour's control of the council, though much later the Liberal Democrats – who emerged from it – did, and in 2004, well after Beecham had stood down as leader, they seized control for seven years.

From the left, the threat was to Beecham personally as well as the party establishment. Councillor Nigel Todd, a pleasant and mild-mannered Marxist, proposed a plan to shift power within the council from Labour councillors to rank-and-file members of the Labour Party outside the council chamber. Among other changes, Beecham's position as leader of the Labour group would have been abolished. Beecham described the reforms as "not compatible with the role of representative democracy".

When Newcastle District Labour Party selected five candidates associated with left-wing groups Militant and the Labour Co-ordinating Committee to stand for the council in 1982, Beecham declared himself unconcerned, and I don't remember any of the five – if they were elected to the council at all – becoming major influences. Labour also safely saw off the threat from the centre-right alliance of Liberals and Social Democrats in 1982, in spite of losing a couple of seats.

Jeremy with Michael Foot, leader of the Labour Party, in 1981.

The Mike Thomas and Nigel Todd initiatives were local symptoms respectively of attempts at national level by the Labour Party's right, led by Roy Jenkins and Shirley Williams, and its left, led by Michael Foot and Tony Benn, to respond to the Margaret Thatcher phenomenon. Beecham avoided aligning himself with either of these factions and focused on keeping Newcastle out of the trouble that was to engulf councils from London to Liverpool in coming years as they attempted to defy government restrictions on their budgets. His strategy was to spend up to the legal maximum on the city's social and other public services while avoiding provoking the government. If ministers' attention was focussed on London and Liverpool, while Newcastle was overlooked, Beecham was, I suspect, quite happy.

There was one change, however, that Labour councillors in the North East could not fend off, though not all wanted to in any case. Following its general election victory in 1983, Mrs Thatcher's second government announced the abolition of the Greater London Council and England's six metropolitan county councils, including Tyne and Wear. The move would restore control over all local government functions to unitary authorities like Newcastle. It was the right decision, Beecham thought, but for the wrong reasons and done in the wrong way.

The government's announcement that Tyne and Wear County Council was to be abolished coincided, roughly, with my own decision to move on from my role specialising in the coverage of local government for the *Chronicle*. But I did have one more occasion to have dealings with Beecham. In my new position as the paper's Chief Reporter, I exposed a scandal involving the abuse of housing improvement grants at the council. Beecham expressed "grave concern and disgust at the exploitation of public funds" and vowed to recover £250,000.

I mention this incident because it exemplifies, along with some other occasions already referred to, one criticism that can justly be made of Beecham's tax-and-spend-to-the-legal-limit approach, which is that the spending was not always well controlled at the micro level. There were numerous reports in those years of over-staffing, excessive bonuses and waste which, if not amounting to much in the grand scheme, might have been expected to undermine public confidence.

Yet they did not dent the Labour vote in the city. In party political terms, the Beecham era was a period of steadily growing and almost unchallenged power for the Labour Party in Newcastle. When the first elections for the new council were held in 1973, Labour won 51 of the 78 seats, with the Conservatives in second place with 23, the Liberals with just one, and three others. By 1994, when Beecham stood down as leader, Labour had 60 councillors, the Liberal Democrats 11 and the Conservatives five. The last Tory election success in the city was in 1992 and four years later there was not a single Conservative councillor, nor has there been since. It was not until ten years after Beecham's leadership, in 2004, that the Liberal Democrats took control, before losing power again to Labour in 2011.

There is one other aspect of council activity where Beecham, looking back, was a disappointment as far as I was concerned, and that is the question of transparency. It is still the case today that important policy decisions in UK local government are taken in the privacy of party group meetings, which in the North East has usually meant in the Labour group. Watching council debates from the public gallery, the naïve might believe they are witnessing an open process, but in fact important decisions have virtually always already been taken. Any councillors who disagree with their group are expected to, and usually do, acquiesce in silence.

This public toeing of the party line has the effect of stifling public debate, especially when the opposition is feeble, as it often has been in the North East. This can have serious consequences, even today, as when four councils in the region – though not Newcastle in this case – made the disastrous decision in 2016 to reject a devolution deal offered by the Government, on the basis of very little open, public debate.

In the 1970s the position was even worse. In defiance of government guidance, committee reports on which important decisions rested were made available to the media only under embargo, meaning their contents could not be published before the meeting at which they were to be discussed and, usually, decided upon. It meant important issues often got no public airing before it was too late. Also in defiance of the guidance, many sub-committee panels and working groups – 19 of them in Newcastle's case – were closed altogether.

Since the 1972 Local Government Act it had only been legal for councils to withhold documents from the media altogether for specified reasons of confidentiality, such as personnel or contractual matters, but Newcastle and other councils managed to interpret this condition widely enough to enable them to withhold virtually anything they wanted on these grounds. This included, in Newcastle's case, all reports and even the agenda of the council's most important committee: the policy and resources committee. Such documents were printed on pink paper, lest anyone should fail to recognise their confidentiality.

In 1976 I conducted my own survey of these practices at 15 councils in the region and reported under the headline 'The hush-hush councils of the North' that eight were defying government guidelines to open up sub-committees as well as committees, and seven, including Newcastle, were imposing embargoes.

When Beecham became Leader of the Council there was, sadly, no improvement in this sorry state of affairs. I reported in January 1981, four years into Beecham's leadership, that councillors had voted to maintain the existing level of secrecy, including the complete behind-closed-doors privacy of the all-important policy and resources committee, consisting of Labour councillors only and chaired by Beecham personally. Councillors got round the problem of the 1972 Act by declaring at the beginning of every meeting that all items on the agenda were of a confidential nature. Looking back, this was probably unlawful and today would certainly be challenged in court. Councils nowadays, including Newcastle, are much more specific about which items of business are confidential and why.

Practice at the time was not just probably unlawful but also deeply hypocritical. Only four months before voting to maintain secrecy at its existing level, councillors had passed a resolution that they were "deeply committed to the principle of giving as much information as possible to the public and Press". The outcome of this triumph of opaque deeds over transparency-promising words was that reporters had to continue relying on leaks to gain access to important information and documents, and this continued to be the case throughout my time as a local government reporter.

I highlighted the hypocrisy and futility of the council's stance at the time by gate-crashing the next meeting of the policy and resources committee, getting duly expelled and reporting these events on the front page of the *Chronicle*, where the leaked 'news you are not supposed to read' was published for all to see. At a personal level, this was much more fun than sitting through what were often boring meetings, and it resulted in what were often matters of little interest receiving front-page treatment. But as a way of conducting council business it was hardly in the public interest. Contrary to the council's rationale for its secrecy, I don't remember any of our leaked reports leading to damage to anyone. None of this made any difference, though. The committee remained closed.

It wasn't just the Press and public who were victim to the culture of secrecy. Rank-and-file councillors were too, even members of the controlling Labour group. The restrictions on information and lack of transparency displayed by both leading councillors and officials towards backbenchers were well documented in a book entitled *Power and Party in an English City: An Account of Single-Party Rule* published in 1981 by David Green, a Newcastle Labour councillor who made the issue his subject of study at Newcastle University. He gave me a copy which I reviewed in the *Chronicle* and which still sits on my shelves.

For 11 years, from 1972 to 1983, my time covering local government for the *Chronicle* had coincided with Beecham's period as a councillor, and for six of those years Beecham was the council leader. Looking back, my overarching impression is of a politician who was professional in the way one expects of the solicitor he was – well organised, well informed, cool-headed, not outwardly passionate or impetuous. He would never give his political opponents an inch but was never anything but courteous, including to me. He was also something of a political loner, owing his long domination of the Labour group and the council to his personal abilities of oratory and mastery of detail rather than membership of a faction. It was this lack of a power base – in a trade union, for example – which I think explains his failure ever to be selected by Labour for a winnable parliamentary seat.

In spite of his lack of outward fervour, Beecham was I believe a sincere fighter for the interests of the most deprived, particularly those of Benwell, the West End and Newcastle as a whole. He stuck to the principles he outlined to me in his 1973 interview to focus on public services, particularly social services, rather than involve himself in the major redevelopment schemes that were turning Newcastle upside down at the time. He taxed and spent to the hilt on these services without getting a reputation as a left-winger, breaching government limits or bringing financial penalties down upon himself, his colleagues or the city. His lack of involvement in big projects ensured that he could avoid any hint of corruption of the type that had marred the Dan Smith era. It is thanks in large part to Beecham that Newcastle came through a period of disruptive physical redevelopment and political and financial turmoil to emerge as the city we see today. But it is a sad irony that many of the social problems that were his main focus in Benwell and other inner-city areas are still with us.

Peter Morris
Journalist

*He possessed the lawyer's unfailing ability
to ask the killer question ...*

One's memory plays tricks and can be selective, often flatteringly
so, particularly when trying to recollect the times and tides of a
seventeen-year working relationship. Nevertheless, memories of the big
ideas and the broad strokes of the 1980s to late 1990s period when our
paths crossed are still clear and warmly remembered.

I came to work for Newcastle City Council Planning Department in
1974 as Assistant City Planning Officer for the east of the city, having
previously worked for Greater Peterborough Development Corporation
on plans to double the size of the town to accommodate London overspill.
At that time, the immediate development priorities were to push ahead
with the major Byker redevelopment and to complete Eldon Square and
the Metro. However, it was not hard to detect that the council's policy focus
was shifting, with a new emphasis on housing renewal, on revitalisation of
the housing stock and with greater priority being given to improving basic
service delivery to the city's residents, particularly education and social
services. I could sense a recoil from the council's earlier development-led
ethos – *Brasilia of The North* etc – and the era of T. Dan Smith. Grand
new development visions were becoming yesterday's news, not only in
Newcastle but nationally.

At that time, Jeremy was the youthful Chair of Social Services, having
been elected to the council in 1977. Together with Derek Webster, the

equally youthful Chair of Education, they formed a dynamic duo, working hand in hand to grow their respective service budgets, political influence and reputations. Jon Davies, Chair of Housing Renewal and the energetic driving force behind the council's housing renewal programme was the third point of the trident. Together they formed a formidable political force, pushing the city forward as a high spending deliverer of good quality, people-centred services. It was hard to resist the new political momentum, despite being under the baleful gaze of the old guard leadership of the council. Inevitably, Jeremy took over as Leader of the Council in 1979, ushering in Newcastle's own 'winds of change' and – little did we know it – the beginning of a working relationship that was to last almost 20 years.

An early manifestation of the new 'top down' political regime was the creation of the 'bottom up' Priority Area Programme, involving local ward councillors working with teams of area-based officers to spend a modest, local ward-based budget on projects that would deliver local benefits and, by working with the local community, help sharpen the leadership's perspective on residents' priorities. This initiative was ground-breaking at the time and was copied, in various forms, by many other local authorities. Most of the initial Priority Area team leaders were area planning officers and I was closely involved in the design and operation of the programme, alongside individuals in the Chief Executive's department.

It became increasingly clear that, with the new political leadership provided by Jeremy, new brooms were going to sweep through the Civic Centre and this would be felt not only politically but also within the council's service departments. Newcastle City Council's organisational structure was characterised by strong service departments and a relatively weak centre. It seemed clear that the new political leadership under Jeremy would also need a much stronger corporate policy-development capacity at the centre of the organisation, together with staff who would act as agents of change to help shake things up and deliver new corporate priorities such as economic development.

The then Chief Executive, Ken Galley, saw the need to respond to the new leader's wishes, but did not want to manage a central staff resource on a day to day basis. Les Elton, the then Deputy Director of Administration and I, two Lancastrian colleagues, were asked to put together and manage a new department to give fresh executive impetus to the leader's requirements. Sadly, Ken Galley died shortly afterwards and in spite of this and despite severe suspicions from service departments, a new Policy Services Department was created in 1980. It is to Jeremy's eternal credit that he provided political cover from the highest level to help bring this new organisational creature to life. Its functions included the council's first Research and Intelligence Unit to improve the evidence base for policy development, and its first Economic Development Unit to drive forward new ideas to regenerate the city's economy. Perhaps most importantly, a handful of bright policy development staff were appointed to provide and monitor a range of new corporate policy approaches, including performance review, European funding and promoting equal opportunities. Whilst somewhat run-of-the-mill these days, some of these innovations were seen as radical 40 years ago.

The new department was very deliberately staffed by a relatively small number of existing officers drawn from service departments. These were people who relished the opportunity to respond to the new political agenda being articulated by the political leadership and who were up for the challenge of being agents of change and of rattling departmental cages. It is interesting how many of these staff, including Jonathan Blackie and Alan Clarke, went on to greater things as chief executives and chief officers of neighbouring local authorities, Heads of regional and government development agencies and including Pat Richie, the council's most recent chief executive whose own council career began in the Economic Development Unit.

The Policy Services Department was very much seen as the cuckoo in the departmental nest. Nevertheless, the resultant friendly fire failed to hold back the production of a wide range of new initiatives, including the council's first Corporate Policy Plan, the promotion of Newcastle as regional capital and the regeneration of Newcastle Quayside.

As a senior officer, I did not look to politicians to write detailed policies or to organise their delivery; I always believed that I was paid to do that. What I looked for was for a coherent vision of what the city could and should be, for an articulation of the political values that should guide the organisation. I also looked for personal application: someone who would read the papers and put the effort in … someone with integrity, intelligence and an ability to delegate and then to support professional staff, especially when the seas got choppy. Above all, he or she needed a deep pride in the city and an openness to new ideas to help promote it. In all of these matters Jeremy was absolutely first class. He also made officers raise their own game: anyone briefing Jeremy had to be on form. At the same time as having a grasp of the big picture, he possessed the lawyer's unfailing ability to ask the killer question.

The latter half of the 1980s saw the winds of change blow once more. In 1986, Les Elton left to become Chief Executive of Gateshead and I was appointed to replace him. The unloved Tyne and Wear County Council was abolished and in 1987 the Tyne and Wear Development Corporation was established. At the same time, Jeremy's reputation as the leading local government politician of his generation inevitably led to his assuming a more prominent national role as Chair of the Association of Metropolitan Authorities. It was a testament to his intelligence and application, not to mention fitness, that he was able to compartmentalise and sustain his ever expanding range of responsibilities without ever breaking step, whilst rushing between the Civic Centre and his professional solicitor's practice in the city.

I observed that even as a politician of principle, Jeremy sometimes needed to look in two directions simultaneously: he would be fiercely promoting Newcastle as one of England's premier regional capitals whilst at the same time arguing relentlessly for a share of every pot of funding going to help alleviate its many social and economic ills. He'd be banging the city's drum with one hand whilst proffering a begging bowl with the other. In this context, the creation of the Tyne and Wear Development Corporation posed a particular dilemma. On the one hand, the imposition of this unelected Tory government body, with its own planning and land acquisition powers, in the very heart of the city, was highly irritating to him. At the same time, Jeremy was persuaded to see that the corporation would bring new resources and investment which would otherwise go elsewhere. My own feelings were more ambivalent. Having worked for a development corporation I could see the benefits of a short term, highly focussed development outfit, unburdened by local democracy and the need to deliver services and with a full set of planning and land acquisition powers. It was clear it would be an eventful relationship and one where we would sometimes both need to face both ways.

It often seemed to me that Jeremy's interests in development projects were primarily aesthetic. He was a sharp and vocal critic of buildings he did not like the look of, or which he felt didn't befit the image of a city such as Newcastle. The new commercial buildings emerging on the Quayside were a particular focus for his displeasure, sometimes rightly so. To my mind, a more significant issue was the use of public money to bribe firms to relocate from the adjacent city centre to the Quayside, leaving behind them empty buildings that, in due course, would become a problem that need to be solved by spending even more public money.

As the 1990s dawned, the winds of change blew once more. Councillors had become increasingly concerned at the fragmentation of the council's development activities across various departments. It was decided to carry out a reorganisation to bring them together under a single chief officer. In 1991 I was asked to establish and lead a new development department to give renewed focus to the council's development and regeneration ambitions. The new department would be overseen by a newly established development committee chaired by Jeremy, who was still Leader of the Council.

The functions of the Policy Services Department were dispersed; it had existed for just over a decade and had done the job it was set up to do … had changed the organisation for the better and created many new initiatives which had been absorbed into the mainstream work of the council. This would not have been possible without the support of Cyril Davies and Geoff Cook, two excellent chief executives and, above all, of Jeremy, whose political leadership provided the fertile ground in which new ideas and initiatives could grow.

The first major job for the development department was to prepare a new development plan for the city, setting the land use, planning and transportation policies for the next 15 years. The city's future depended on reversing the trend of declining population, creating new economic opportunity and enhancing the quality of its environment. The city needed to attract new investment and jobs not only in its own interests but also in the interests of the region of which it was undoubtedly the capital. The draft plan, signed by Jeremy as Leader of the Council, was published in 1991 for widespread public consultation. The plan's proposals were radical and controversial in proposing a major extension of the city's built-up area into the green belt, beyond the Western Bypass, to provide new housing and strategic employment sites.

Jeremy and I always thought we could win the inevitable main argument at the forthcoming public inquiry. If it were to grow, the city could only ever expand to the west and north. Newcastle's very tight green belt was more of a 'green noose' slowly strangling the city. The city lacked sites of sufficient quality to attract footloose inward investment, and many workers who wanted to live in the city were forced to burn fuel, clogging up the commuter routes twice daily, because Newcastle itself could not provide enough new housing. The option of building on every scrap of open land in the city, brownfield or otherwise, would be too damaging to the local environment. Although we didn't realise it at the time, we were advancing a case largely based on sustainability arguments, twenty years before they became fashionable. The plan's proposals provoked a lot of reaction, including from neighbouring local authorities. After a long public inquiry the inspector found in our favour. We had won the argument, and the new Unitary Development Plan for the city was finally approved by the Secretary of State in 1993. At the time, it was the UK's largest green belt incursion.

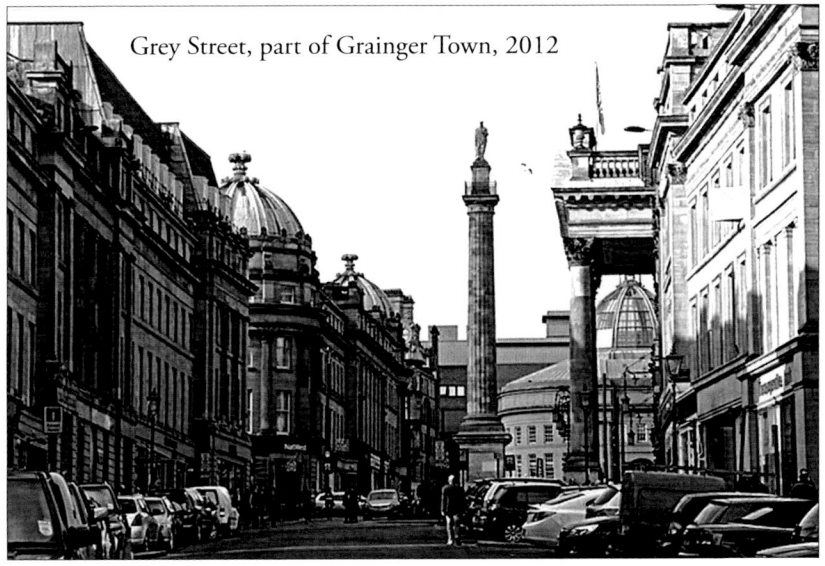

Grey Street, part of Grainger Town, 2012

Our next major challenge was the regeneration of Grainger Town in the heart of the city. The area was the city's shop front to the world, with one of the biggest concentrations of listed buildings in England. When many people conjure up an image of Newcastle as the regional capital they see Grey Street rising up to the majestic Grey's Monument. However, the area was increasingly characterised by the flight of occupiers and investment, by property vacancy and by a degrading environment. Grainger Town had to be regenerated. It was not only a Newcastle heritage asset, it was also a conservation area of national importance. We made a powerful case to government and in 1993 Newcastle was invited by English Heritage to prepare an action plan and establish the Grainger Town Partnership to bid for English Heritage and national conservation grants. It was always recognised that reversing the decline of Grainger Town, even though a long and painstaking process, was a major challenge that simply had to be met. Indeed, it still continues today. However, I think that initiating the project remains one of the best memories for Jeremy and me.

Of the many big schemes and initiatives, such as the regeneration of both Newburn Haugh and Walker Riverside, one of the most memorable episodes of that time was the fight to accommodate the ambitious stadium development plans of Newcastle United. After a journey that involved many twists and turns – not to mention the odd ambush – the successful outcome is there for all to see, with St James' Park appreciated as one of the nation's best sporting venues. As a longstanding NUFC season ticket holder, it's an outcome of which I expect Jeremy is very thankful.

Jeremy stepped down as Leader of the Council in 1994. His role chairing the development committee was very ably carried on by David Slesenger. Although remaining a local councillor for the Benwell ward, it was becoming increasingly clear that his national roles and his leadership of the Association of Metropolitan Authorities were demanding ever more of his time. After some 23 years with Newcastle City Council, I left in 1997, the same year Jeremy assumed leadership of the Local Government Association.

I came to Newcastle in 1974 having helped double the size of Peterborough, without the help of any local politicians. Jeremy and other fine councillors such as Roy Burgess quickly helped dispel any jaundiced notions I might have had about local political leadership. Jeremy was the finest local government politician of his generation, as his rise to national prominence and eventually the House of Lords testifies. I valued our professional working relationship and friendship. I admired his political vision, his integrity, eloquence and intelligence. I enjoyed working with him. It was a privilege and, for almost all of the time, it was a pleasure!

Roy Ashton
Newcastle City Council: Assistant City Planning Officer (1974-1980), Head of Policy Planning (1980-86), Head of Policy Services (1986-1991) and Director of Development (1991-97).

*New brooms were needed, and Jeremy was one of them.*

Jeremy has retired as a councillor after 55 years of public service to the people of Benwell, Benwell & Scotswood and the city of Newcastle upon Tyne. It is an extraordinary achievement. Coupled with all his leadership roles nationally, his knighthood, his peerage and his Freedom of the City of Newcastle upon Tyne, it is a record unequalled by anyone.

After Oxford, Jeremy returned to Newcastle and joined the legal practice of Alan Henderson, a well-known solicitor in Newcastle with offices on Blackett Street and then Collingwood Street. Alan was a long-standing friend of my aunt and uncle who lived in Gosforth, a friendship which went back to the 1930s and the days of the Independent Labour Party. I recall many chats with Alan during my teenage years. He was a radical in terms of social justice though a firm believer in the punishment fitting the crime. One day, I recall him telling my aunt that he was very proud to have recruited a young solicitor to his practice who had been at the Royal Grammar School, then University College Oxford, where he had chaired the Labour Club and had recently become a councillor in Newcastle. Alan believed Jeremy would have a very bright political future at the highest levels.

I moved to Newcastle with Margaret in 1969 after graduation to work in brand management at Procter & Gamble. Shortly afterwards in the autumn of that year, Alan invited us for coffee one Sunday morning to meet Jeremy and Brenda. Alan knew that I had political ambitions but without much practical form; Newcastle seemed a desert for Liberals. That changed a few years later as we began to make inroads against the two main parties and I was elected a councillor in Gosforth. I remember listening to Jeremy talk about the city and I recall thinking that here was a man with a social mission to address economic decline, poverty and inequality. He also knew that the Labour Party needed to recover from the T. Dan Smith era. Its reputation in Newcastle had been tarnished following his leadership between 1960 and 1965. New brooms were needed, and Jeremy was one of them.

When Jeremy was elected to the City Council in 1967, he joined a team of dedicated councillors and talented officers who were re-engineering the city – smoke control, slum clearance, the central motorway, planning the Metro, new council housing, the design of Eldon Square shopping centre. It was an exciting time. The council bought the Theatre Royal in 1971 for just £185,000 to save it from closing and Jeremy was instrumental in ensuring it had the resources to grow back to its previous pre-eminence inside the public sector. It is often said that the role of the public sector is to correct market failure; this was a classic example. Six years later, the Royal Shakespeare Company announced Newcastle Theatre Royal as a third home alongside Stratford and the Barbican.

Jeremy had chaired the Social Services Committee from 1973 until 1977 when he took over as leader of the Labour group and thus of the City Council. It was a crucial period for the creation of a new social services department in Newcastle following the Social Services Act (1970) which implemented the Seebohm Report of the previous year. I joined the committee as a new Liberal councillor in 1975 and was immediately struck by Jeremy's leadership in tandem with Bryan Roycroft, one of the country's leading directors of social services. Under their leadership, Newcastle became an exemplar council for unifying its care provision in support of the welfare and health of adults and of children and for being the first council to achieve a fully qualified workforce.

Seebohm had urged a "more coherent pattern of care provision for elderly people including early identification". The Social Services Act had in turn created the framework for a single social services department emphasising the need for a "coordinated and comprehensive approach to social care, supporting families, and encouraging people to seek help". It is because of Jeremy's visionary leadership that Newcastle achieved its preeminent position in the field. The resources were made available and when in opposition before 1973, Jeremy had, with colleagues, worked out the delivery plan. When he became the leader in 1977 and Chair of the Policy and Resources Committee, he also took over as the chair of the Finance Committee, thereby ensuring the social services department continued to receive the resources it needed.

Jeremy also gave a practical outcome to the ambition of encouraging people to seek help. He established the Welfare Rights Service with dedicated council staff whose job was to increase the take-up of benefits by those who, for whatever reason, did not claim their entitlement. Working closely with Citizens Advice, he built up an impressive resource which helped to strengthen families and neighbourhoods.

As a councillor for Benwell, he was involved in the establishment of the Benwell Community Development Project in 1972, one of twelve such projects across the country. It was time-limited for six years and from it grew the West End Resource Centre and the Newcastle Law Centre. It gave information and advice on demand to individuals. It intervened to give practical welfare rights and legal help, simplify forms, help build neighbourhoods and, through its Big Ideas Group (BIG), it set in train the concept of 'priority areas' which were introduced early in Jeremy's leadership. Jeremy was right that pump-priming comparatively small sums of money helped to build neighbourhoods coping with poverty and poor housing. However, he had to face opposition from areas – many of them poor but locked within better-off areas – which were denied this source of funding. In time, however, all poorer areas were allocated extra support.

During Jeremy's period of leadership, there were two national censuses completed in 1981 and 1991. Jeremy produced city profiles showing all the key data at both a city and ward level which to this day makes important reading. In his introduction to the 1981 *City Profiles* (published in 1983), Jeremy wrote a terse message about rising unemployment and the decline of traditional industries. He challenged the government to make "radical changes … in policy" and to ensure through its policies and grants that it would reverse "the grim record of decline in employment prospects". He did, however, point to the improvements in housing conditions of recent years in the city and he also spotted a key fact which underpinned all his future strategic thinking about the need for growth in the city to offset the problems caused by Newcastle having "one of the highest proportions of retired people, and one of the lowest proportions of young families" of all the metropolitan areas of England. He was proved right.

*City Profiles* was published again after the 1991 census. The foreword was longer and contained an even more bleak message. He talked of Newcastle being a poorer city, an increasingly ageing city, and one which was "an increasingly unequal city in an increasingly unequal country". Jeremy was not someone who gave up in the face of adversity. The prospect of a Labour government was getting stronger. He just worked harder to improve the lot of his city and its residents.

In his tussle with Mrs Thatcher's government over revenue support for the city, Jeremy did make a surprising decision – to increase the rates to make up for government cuts. There was a national debate on whether councils should have the powers to increase local taxes, including business rates, to whatever level they wanted. Businesses were aghast at what they were facing and demanded greater efficiency in local spending – a reasonable request. Poor people also need low levels of taxation. Labour lost the narrative here, and it dented people's confidence in them, seeing Labour as a high-tax party not delivering good value for money.

Jeremy had fought the 1970 General Election in Tynemouth. He aspired to a parliamentary career, and he would have gone far as a minister, but this was the election that Ted Heath won in the last few days with his promise to "cut prices at a stroke". It was unachievable, as voters later discovered. That, coupled with the sitting MP being the redoubtable Dame Irene Ward, led to Jeremy losing by just under seven thousand votes. He deserved better and was to try for a safer seat at the next general election, but it didn't happen – to the lasting benefit of our city.

He said on several occasions over the next twenty years that he could never have achieved as much as he did as Leader of Newcastle City Council if he had become an MP. For one thing, the Conservatives were in power for most of them. For another, as leader of a major city he could decide things and drive change. He ended up in a very strong position when Labour won in 1997. He understood the machinery of government and he knew what he wanted to do. Others would heed his advice.

As a councillor, Jeremy was a familiar sight walking between his office in Collingwood Street and the Civic Centre. He must have held the world record for his speed up Northumberland Street. Anyone wishing to raise an issue would never have been able to keep up!

Jeremy was always sensitive to any possible challenge to his position as leader. In 1978, Councillor Tom Collins, who had been Lord Mayor the previous year, challenged Jeremy for the leadership; Tom had been the leader from 1973 to 1977 and wanted to return. Jeremy held on by one vote. I was surprised by the tight margin because I had assumed the baton had been passed on willingly by the old guard. Not at all, and Jeremy had to contend with the continued opposition of East End councillors and politicians over many years. Newcastle had managed to unite its east and west end football teams a century before, but it has proved a step too far for some East End Labour politicians.

Jeremy belonged to the Labour tribe. He rejected the SDP led by the Gang of Four in 1981, preferring to fight from within the Labour Party to wrest control from the left.

The Newcastle caretakers' strike that lasted over six weeks from January to early March 1979 was not the council's finest hour. It demonstrated the complexities for leaders trying to find speedy solutions to complex issues without the benefit of hindsight. Caretakers went on strike over terms and conditions, schools were closed, and head teachers did not cover the caretakers' duties. Parents became understandably angry at their children's lack of learning. Jeremy did his best and lots of meetings were held and lots of press releases were issued. We all thought the strike would be sorted out within days and then within a few more days but this was the winter of discontent and it dragged on. On 3 March, two separate demonstrations clashed outside St James' Park – 400 from seventeen different Newcastle parent teachers' associations and a counter demonstration in support of the caretakers who accused the PTAs of holding a strike-breaking march. I concluded at the time – and still do – that Jeremy was between a rock and a hard place. Things could have been worse, but the outcome was a public perception that Labour put the interests of trade unions before the public interest. And Mrs Thatcher became Prime Minister just two months later.

Jeremy tended towards democratic centralism, believing that only national government could equalise wealth and opportunity and provide the resources and the direction that enabled local areas to succeed. He never seemed comfortable with the concept of Liberals as a third force in British politics and made this clear on several occasions when I heard him speak. Two parties were enough. The trouble was that the public increasingly began to see the Liberals in their various forms (Alliance, Liberal Democrat) as a party of the future. Most of the Labour Party in Newcastle never woke up to the threat we Liberals posed but in the mid-1980s, once the SDP had been launched and had done badly in local polls, he wrote a memo to the Labour Group which was leaked to the Evening Chronicle in which he pointed to the Liberal Party's growth in number of councillors and how Labour had to stop us, not the SDP. For twenty years, Labour held us off without any real difficulty but after 1997, once Labour was in power in Westminster, the cracks began to show. In 2004 Labour lost control of the city to us by a wide margin (18 seats). His warning had proved prescient.

Labour tended towards the conservative in how it operated. When

Jeremy took over as Chair of Policy and Resources Committee in 1977, press and public – and opposition councillors – were excluded from meetings as they always had been. Labour saw no case for change. It is hard to imagine given today's world of open access to information, yet despite requests from us and despite stern leaders in the *Evening Chronicle*, this practice just carried on. Decisions of major importance were being made behind closed doors; it had to stop. By the mid-1980s, Councillor Mike Cookson and I realised we had to attend a meeting and not shift when asked to. This we did and the meeting was moved somewhere else but over the next few weeks Labour found itself on the wrong side of public opinion. The Policy and Resources Committee was finally opened up to the public, although any commercially sensitive items remained (rightly) on a closed agenda as they are today. Strangely, the press statement announcing this change of heart was handled by Deputy Leader Roy Burgess. Had Jeremy supported change all along?

As a councillor for 55 years, Jeremy saw many new initiatives come and go. All shared a common objective – to improve the lot of deprived communities: Housing Action Areas, General Improvement Areas, Inner City Partnership, City Challenge, Single Regeneration Budget, Housing Market Renewal. They all helped, but it proved impossible to eliminate the impact of low incomes. He was right to think that central government should provide the resources so that local government could get on with the job. He coined the phrase "Grow or we die". He knew Newcastle had to be bigger; it needed more council tax and business rate income. He knew this meant expanding the city northwest across the Western Bypass. I was dubious at first, preferring to think in terms of redeveloping the inner city. In the end, it became obvious that we had to do both, and during my own period of leadership, this is what we did. The Newcastle Great Park never quite turned out as hoped for by the planners in the 1990s – lots of jobs near residential areas, cycles for all, green and sustainable living – but the intention was good and the design quality was good. Jeremy had a particular obsession with design quality. I recall one delightful meeting when the Highways Agency was hauled over the coals for the poor design of the Western Bypass – too much brutalist concrete and an absence of decorative elements! He was right of course and they added a few stripes.

Jeremy needed all his political skills to manage the consequences of the creation of the Tyne and Wear Development Corporation in 1987. This was the brainchild of Michael Heseltine who believed state intervention was the key to the renewal of Newcastle Quayside. He also believed local government was not the vehicle for delivering the economic step-change needed. The government-appointed agency (like several others across England) had a membership drawn from the local community but appointed by the Secretary of State. It led to accusations of undemocratic decision-making and poor investment decisions. This latter objection was hard to justify as anyone looking at the Newcastle Gateshead Quayside today would agree; it is a terrific achievement. That decisions were reached in an undemocratic way was partly true; local councils were sidelined. Michael Heseltine wanted real outcomes and he got them – and very quickly. As one senior member of the council (not Jeremy) said to me, "John, if the money had come to the council, they would have spent it on social services."

It's important to remember what Jeremy achieved from all the money that arrived to gap-fund and kick-start schemes on the Quayside: land prepared for new development and jobs, investment in new industries, substantial subsidies for off-shore industries. There was a social housing programme and a skills-training programme that helped several thousand local residents to train and retrain. There was also a cultural programme for community projects.

Sitting one evening in the Chamber of the House of Lords, it was one of those memorable moments when Jeremy and Michael Heseltine exchanged mutual congratulations on each being "someone I could work with" all those years ago. They were indeed, and the Tyne benefited hugely.

Jeremy had led the city for seventeen years when he decided in 1994 to hand over the leadership and to concentrate his efforts at a national level.

He was still working professionally, and he had been elected Chair of the Association of Metropolitan Authorities three years previously. He set off to lead the amalgamation of the three local government associations (Metropolitan, County and District) into a single, stronger body. It was a task that would have defeated most, but Jeremy's skills at consulting, planning, and fixing shone through. He succeeded brilliantly and became the first leader of the Local Government Association in 1997. It was of course a productive time to be a Labour politician, full of potential for schools, health and care, and community services. Local government would no longer be the poor relation in the eyes of central government once Labour achieved power under Tony Blair. Jeremy then carried a crucial responsibility for speaking to central government on behalf of local government. That so much happened after 1997 to address the funding problems that Jeremy had fought to redress over thirty years was in large measure because he was local government's power broker with Number 10.

Today's structure of local government – that is, the cabinet and scrutiny model – owes much to Jeremy. I have never felt that such a model played to the strengths of councillors, who are part-time volunteers representing a ward, and not full-time politicians; backbench and opposition councillors mostly prefer the committee system which gives them something to do. I do as well, but I acknowledge that local government became more streamlined, and decisions were taken more quickly. Scrutiny, however, has always been the poor relation because councillors have found it difficult to challenge officers with their professional knowledge.

On 6 May 1977, with Jeremy about to become Council Leader and with Hugh White as Lord Mayor, the US President, Jimmy Carter flew into Newcastle at the start of his first visit to the UK. Why did he land in Newcastle? Well, it was politically neutral – not being Wales or Scotland – and was well away from other cities closer to London. It also had a decent runway! Jimmy Carter was from Georgia and had been inaugurated in January that year having been elected on an anti-Washington ticket. The

PM, James Callaghan, decided that Newcastle fitted the bill in so many ways. He also knew that Newcastle had first-rate, reliable leadership that would deliver a successful start to President Carter's visit to the UK – which it most certainly did.

President Jimmy Carter visited Newcastle on 6 May 1977.
He greeted an 80,000 strong crowd at the Civic Centre with
"Howay the lads".

One outcome of the visit was the creation of the Rosalyn Carter Friendship Force and the twinning of Newcastle with Atlanta. Exchanges proliferated, friendships were made, and the concept expanded to other places. One direct outcome was the selection of Newcastle by the Foreign Office, along with Coventry, to spearhead twinning relationships with an emergent China. Newcastle was invited to twin with Taiyuan, a coal and steel producing area in Shanxi province 300 miles west of Beijing. In 1985 Jeremy led the first delegation, where he seriously impressed his hosts with his detailed knowledge of Confucius! The importance of this link with China must not be underestimated; it was a critical arm of UK foreign policy as China searched for more friendly relations and improved trade and investment. I was on the delegation the following year supporting the Lord Mayor, Roy Burgess, and I recall vividly our briefing in the British Embassy on arrival in China. We were hoping to push on with a power station order for Reyrolle Parsons, but the Embassy's absolute priority was that we would state and re-state the words 'Now the Hong Kong question is settled'. We did – beaming the message to millions of viewers on nightly TV news channels.

Jeremy was awarded a peerage in 2010. When it was announced (mine was announced at the same time) he and I received a standing ovation at the next council meeting. I couldn't see his face because colleagues were in the way but I can imagine he felt and looked very proud. He deserved to. He stayed on the council until his retirement in 2022. Some felt this was beyond the call of duty given his front bench roles in local government and justice in London, but Jeremy wanted to keep in touch with the people and neighbourhoods he knew and to reflect them in his work in London. He retired from the House of Lords in 2021, giving space to other local government colleagues to take over.

Jeremy stands in the great tradition of local government leaders. He was a brilliant speaker, noted for his wit whatever the occasion. He once dubbed David Faulkner and me "The Likely Lads". I found it very funny until I realised that I didn't know which one was me! He loved the opportunities council meetings gave him for having a go at the Opposition and when the Conservatives disappeared he tried very hard to have a go at us. He was less successful in that, despite asking me if I would raise the temperature of council meetings. As I pointed out to him, we debated issues and were not tribal over them. Anyway, we could not let Labour occupy all the anti-Tory ground in the 1990s.

Jeremy was also a brilliant thinker. Look at the committee structure under his leadership. Note the Regional Capital sub-committee or the Land Strategy sub-committee. I belonged to most of these committees as the Opposition member and wanted to be there because they were in practice the engine rooms for change.

Over the thirty years of Labour administration from 1974 to 2004 and then again from 2011, Jeremy was right at the heart of everything that happened at Newcastle City Council. Other councillors such as Roy Burgess, Jon Davies, Tony Flynn, Joan Lamb, Danny Marshall, David Slesenger, Derek Webster and Hugh White, with many others, played critical roles in supporting Jeremy.

Nevertheless, the truth is that Jeremy led from the front, and in so doing he changed our city for the better.

John Shipley
The Lord Shipley OBE

*London calling ...*

"His dedication to local communities across the country has been tireless and his many years in the House of Lords has allowed him to continue doing what he does best – standing up for people and trying to make things better for us all. Everyone in local government holds him in the highest regard and we thank him for his dedication."

LGA Chairman, Councillor James Jamieson,
responding to the announcement that Lord Jeremy Beecham
would be retiring as a councillor in May 2022.

*His contributions to civic life in Newcastle and its suburbs are truly remarkable ...*

Other contributors to this volume have celebrated Jeremy Beecham's outstanding leadership of Newcastle City Council from 1977-1994, as well as his 55 years of service as a dedicated local councillor.  Here I want to offer a personal reflection on Jeremy's approach to civic leadership and community improvement when viewed from outside Newcastle.  It is, however, helpful to start my tribute in Newcastle, as this is where I first met Jeremy.

**The Newcastle/Gateshead Inner City Partnership (1977-1979)**

In June 1977, the then Labour Government launched a bold, new urban programme: *Policy for the Inner Cities.*  This national strategy was designed to give inner city areas an explicit social and economic priority, and seven 'partnership areas' were invited to prepare Inner Area Programmes.  One of these was the Newcastle/Gateshead Inner City Partnership.  In a move that was unusual at the time, government ministers chaired and participated in Inner City Partnership meetings in the designated cities.

As Team Leader of the Gateshead Inner Area Programme at the time, I attended the Newcastle/Gateshead Partnership meetings in 1977-79.  I have a strong memory of the new, fresh-faced leader of Newcastle City Council addressing the first meeting and making an immediate and positive impact on the direction of the debate. In these meetings with ministers, Jeremy was not simply an articulate advocate for his city; he also demonstrated a great understanding of the challenges that the inner city communities north and south of the River Tyne were experiencing.

From the 'get go' he actively made the case for expanding the role and influence of elected local authorities in shaping national urban policy. Even at this early stage in his career Jeremy was clear that central/local partnerships could improve the effectiveness of public policy – always provided the partnership is not modelled on, as he put it, "the rider and the horse"![1]

## Leadership of the Local Government Association (1997-2004)

Some twenty years after leaving Newcastle I had the good fortune to have further contact with Jeremy when, in 1997, he became the leading national voice for local government in our country. In 1991 Jeremy had already become Chairman of the Association of Metropolitan Authorities (AMA), and his outstanding record of public service was recognised in 1994 when he was knighted. Jeremy went on to play a key role in creating the Local Government Association (LGA) and was the first chairman of this new national body, serving as its chair from 1997-2004.

The Labour government, elected in 1997, was keen to reform and improve local government and Jeremy was an influential figure in the development of a range of national efforts to strengthen local democracy. Various reforms were introduced quite quickly, including the creation, in 2000, of a new Greater London Authority, led by a directly elected mayor. The Local Government Act 2000 gave new powers to local government and required most local authorities to shift from their traditional committee-based system of decision-making to an executive model, possibly with a directly elected mayor.

1 J. Beecham (1979) 'Problems and opportunities of partnership: a political perspective' in T. A. Broadbent (ed) *Inner area partnerships and programmes: the first year's experience*. Policy Series 8, p.69   London: Centre for Environmental Studies

I was an academic adviser to ministers at this time, and partly because I had studied city leadership models in other countries, I was invited to facilitate exchanges between UK local government leaders and US-based directly elected mayors. I recall an occasion in 1999 when Jeremy demonstrated his ability to act in a most statesmanlike and constructive way on the international stage. It is well known that Jeremy was not an enthusiast for the directly elected mayor model of local governance; he favoured more collective approaches to civic leadership. However, he was always keen to examine the evidence and to consider new possibilities.

At a UK/US seminar on *Models of Local Government* held in London on 5/6 October 1999, Jeremy facilitated, alongside Nick Raynsford – then Minister for London and Construction – a high-level exchange between a group of senior US city mayors and a group of senior UK local government leaders. I recall Jeremy's enthusiasm for teasing out the strengths and weaknesses of different ways of making decisions and, not surprisingly, he created warm relationships with our transatlantic visitors.

At the reception, held at the US Embassy at the end of the international exchange, Jeremy stood alongside then US Ambassador Philip Lader, and won everyone over, including Ambassador Lader, with his wit and charm. He was in sparkling form, and, in his opening remarks, he explained that the last time he had been in Grosvenor Square was at the famous anti-Vietnam War protest held in March 1968!

Jeremy has many strengths, and his contributions to civic life in Newcastle and its suburbs are truly remarkable. In addition, he has played an enormously important national role in advancing the cause not just of delivering social and economic justice in Britain, but also for strengthening local democracy.

Robin Hambleton
Emeritus Professor of City Leadership at the University of the West of England, Bristol

"His local and national legacy – whether the hugely successful Quids for Kids campaign in Newcastle, tackling poverty through innovative Priority Area Teams in the city, persuading Gordon Brown to introduce free concessionary travel for pensioners, or successfully campaigning for educational maintenance grants to help children from disadvantaged backgrounds stay in education – have transformed the lives of thousands. His personal modesty means his achievements have often been under-recognised, but there's no doubt he's been one of the great transforming politicians of modern times."

Councillor Nick Forbes
Leader of Newcastle City Council 2011-2022

*Jeremy Beecham stands outs as the brightest*
*and the best of them ...*

In 1984 the Conservative government introduced legislation to limit council spending; this became known as 'rate-capping'. Over the ensuing two years Labour councils attempted to deal with the consequences of this, and a number of them tried collectively to challenge the Government. They failed in this, and from the chaos of that defeat a new approach emerged in local government that focused on delivering good services economically, which was to see Labour become the dominant party in local government across much of the country.

At that time, I was working in the private office of Ken Livingstone who was leading the Greater London Council; I was a councillor in Lewisham, one of the rate-capped boroughs. Labour councils and their leaders met again and again to try and find a coherent response and it was at one of these meetings that I first encountered Jeremy Beecham, who by then had been Leader of Newcastle City Council for seven years. He was one of a cadre of younger leaders of northern Labour councils who were beginning to change the way those councils worked.

While some of us tested theories about the power of local democracy to destruction, Jeremy was a calm voice taking a longer view. I didn't know then how closely I would work with him in the years that followed, but despite being part of a group of young, London Labour councillors impatient for change it was already clear to me that Jeremy was someone who was going to be a significant figure at the national level.

We found ourselves serving together on the Association of Metropolitan Authorities Policy Committee – a Labour-dominated body which represented the big cities. It was initially controlled by an elderly leadership but the emergence of leaders like Jeremy, and David Blunkett in Sheffield, were making it clear that change was coming. The rest of the country tended to regard colleagues from London with some suspicion but perhaps because of my northern roots I managed to build a good working relationship with Jeremy and the rest as things moved to the point where he became the AMA Leader.

Jeremy was now a key figure in both local government and the Labour Party. He was tough, clear-minded and imaginative, with an extraordinary range of skills and a powerful intellect. It was his leadership that made the creation of a single local government association for England possible. The existence of three separate associations had made it difficult to hold coherent conversations with the Government, almost inviting it to 'divide and conquer'. I remember a private meeting one evening at a London hotel when a number of leaders from across English local government listened to colleagues from Scotland describe how very different the relationships were for their single, united local government association … and to Jeremy's persuasive words that followed.

Many said it simply wouldn't happen, but it did, and Jeremy was the driving force behind it. It was therefore entirely appropriate that he should lead the new body and become the voice of English local government. By now I had served as Leader of Lewisham but had returned to the back benches to pursue a career outside local government. However, as the arrangements to set up the new body – to be called the Local Government Association – were being made, it was decided that each national political party should be funded to have a private office within the LGA in order to engage with councillors elected in all parts of the country for that particular party, to manage the internal politics that are important to all such groups.

Thus I found myself sitting in front of people who had been political colleagues not long before and being interviewed for the role of setting up, and then running, the Labour political office that would support Sir Jeremy and his colleagues. Jeremy was persuaded that I could help make the new organisation succeed, so for the next five years we were to work very closely together.

During this time I saw a different side to Jeremy's approach. By nature, he wanted to get people working together; despite his toughness he was never one to enjoy confrontation. He was someone for whom it was a genuine pleasure to work – he gave you the time and opportunity to do what needed to be done. And while there were, of course, times when someone in my role needed to 'fix' things, this was always easier to achieve because of the huge respect there was for Jeremy across local government and within the Labour Party.

The Local Government Association owes a great deal to Jeremy's hard work, clear vision and intellectual leadership during those early years. His success was such that the LGA became part of the wider political landscape in a way that the previous associations had never been. It was only when I was working with him on a daily basis that I fully understood just what a thoughtful leader Jeremy was. Politics is all too often about the short term but Jeremy knew the importance of taking the long view, and learning how to do that was immensely valuable to me personally when I left the LGA to become Lewisham's first elected executive mayor. A few years later I found myself as one of London's representatives on the LGA Policy Committee and when the need arose to take the association's human resources work in a fresh direction I was honoured when Jeremy asked me to lead that work. Once again, I learned how good it was working with this man – he gave you free rein to do what was needed, only asking that he be kept properly briefed. It wasn't Jeremy's way to interfere or micro-manage, but he was always ready to help work through potential solutions to complex problems.

It has been a pleasure and a privilege to have worked with, and for, Jeremy Beecham through the years but there is one characteristic of his that I must mention in closing: Jeremy is a genuinely funny man – his humour can disarm and entertain. His speeches rarely failed to have at least one very good and original joke and others who were less gifted in that way were happy to borrow from him when the need arose.

I have been fortunate to have worked with some outstanding local government leaders through the years, but Jeremy Beecham stands out as the brightest and the best of them – his achievements deserve to be celebrated, and at a time when huge challenges face our nation he reminds one that integrity, honesty and vision really can make a lasting difference at every level of government.

Sir Steve Bullock DL

# MEMORIES OF A LIFE IN POLITICS

**Edited transcript of an interview with Judith Green
recorded at Jeremy's home in Gosforth on 16 February 2020.**

*Can you tell me briefly about your political career and how you got involved in the Labour Party. You weren't born into it, were you?*
Well, I was actually. My paternal grandmother, who died about ten years before I was born, was a member of the Communist Party – it was called something else but it became the Communist Party – pre First World War. And my father was always a Labour supporter. My first political memory was in the 1951 election, when I was six, because I woke up in the morning and the radio was giving the status of the parties, and at that point we were in the lead. And I said, "That's good", and my brother said, "Oh no, because it's not by enough. These results will give us more Tory MPs". In those days the early results tended to be urban and so the Tory results came in and we lost the election. And that was my first political memory. But I was genetically affiliated to the Labour Party from the very beginning.

And in the '59 election my father did a bit of driving for the election, and I joined the Party on my fifteenth birthday. And I have remained ever since, notwithstanding some temptations.

And so I started a Young Socialists Branch in the ward, and I was secretary of Jesmond Ward, and so on. And at Oxford I became chairman of the Labour Club at the university. And when I got back I worked in local elections – and I did in Oxford as well actually. And I stood the first time as a councillor in Arthur's Hill Ward in Newcastle, in 1965 it must have been, when I was 21 – against Arthur Grey who was the leader of Newcastle City Council at the time. And later I became a councillor for Benwell. It was the adjoining ward to the one I'd done most work in, because Elswick Ward was very marginal in those days, and that was the ward I tended to do work in. So I didn't know Benwell but it was near enough to be familiar in some respects. And of course, at that time, it was pretty dreadful in Benwell. It's got huge problems now but they're not as visibly obvious as they were then, because there were some houses in terrible conditions in the ward. So for somebody from a comfortable middle class family it was a shock, I suppose you would say.

**Can you talk more about the problems?**

Well, a lot of the housing was dire. I mean it was privately rented – slums actually, a lot of it. That was the main thing. And a lot of overcrowding. And it was just dreadful. There were few local amenities, and the services generally were pretty poor.

I remember where you had houses with three storeys, and an outside loo and a basin on the landing. It was just horrendous. It wasn't all as bad as that, but that was pretty much the worst. And of course we'd only had a Labour Council once before – in '45 to '48. And it was then from '58 that we had a Labour council after that. And of course predominantly since then, with the exception of the Lib-Dem interval, we've had a Labour council except when I got on, because my arrival coincided with the Tories taking over for the first time as a Tory council, because they used to stand as Progressives – misleading description of them – before then. So I came on and it coincided with the Tories taking over.

**When you were leaving university did you ever think of not coming back to Newcastle?**

No … not at all.

### *To go to London?*

No, no. Even though I wasn't born here. My father was at a munitions factory at Leicester during the war and they came back to Newcastle. So since the age of two.

### *How did you come to be selected for Benwell?*

I can't remember if I'd actually canvassed in Benwell before. I think Connie Lewcock, who was the councillor, I think she may have suggested me. She was wonderful. So there I was. I can't remember who was up against me. Connie and Tom Yellowley of course were the other councillors …

### *When did Dan Smith take over, then?*

He took over about '58 as leader of the Labour Group. And he wasn't leader for that long actually. It was only about six years. I think it was '64 he stood down, something like that. Because he had his other interests, didn't he?

### *When you look back, bearing in mind that obviously his memory still taints the Labour Party in Newcastle, and that if you go to other parts of the country and mention Newcastle, Dan Smith is what everybody talks about …*

Still? Fifty years on?

### *… leaving aside that he broke the law and brought the Labour Party into disrepute, how would you consider Smith's career as the Labour Party leader in Newcastle and what he achieved?*

The first thing to say is that he was a *leader*, which was a fairly new thing really for local government in many ways, to have a strong and – to say 'visionary' might be to stretch it a bit – but anyway, with ideas and promoting ideas and pushing for change. We hadn't had that happen in Newcastle. The most exciting thing in Newcastle politics was when someone made off with some fire engines during the Second World War.

Really nothing of any significance was done until we took control in the fifties. And the housing thing was absolutely upfront. But the concept of the city as a major part of the country, its potential, hadn't existed before. It was just small town stuff really, until then. And so, visibly through housing, and other measures as well, it began to kick off, I suppose, in the sixties. And there was a different feel to the place from what had been a fairly sleepy provincial town. It didn't have a city feel really, looking back, in the sense that developed from the sixties on. And Smith, for all his faults, deserves some recognition for that.

*At some level, did that inspire you?*
Well, he had gone from the council by the time I arrived, so it wasn't a personal thing. But the fact was that it was apparent from the age of 15 to me that things in Newcastle would have to change. Too many people were living in dire conditions. Mind you, we continue to say that, but it takes a slightly different form. Yes, I mean it was evident, and I felt drawn into trying to promote the changes that would help transform people's lives. That's what good local government should be about.

*Did you ever know Dan Smith personally?*
He was charismatic. His defects didn't emerge until some time later. It was sad, it was very sad. And damaging of course for the state of the Labour Party – and for the city as well. But, he got the city moving. Nothing had happened, as I said, in local government for decades until we took office in '58 under his leadership.

*Were you impressed by the fact that he had the courage to face down opposition, do a lot of unpopular things like demolishing half of Sandyford to create the education precinct, rather than back off when faced with vocal opposition?*
You have to remember I wasn't on the council when he was on the council, so I wasn't closely involved in any of the stuff. I was merely a

Party member at that time. And what was evident was that he was driving change in the city. And that seemed to me fine. I don't recall the detail of things which other people might not have liked, but you always get that. Change is not going to be approved of by the entire population. I didn't see him debating in the chamber, but he was a very good speaker. He was not a typical local councillor as is generally defined. He was a leader in a way that, at that time, wasn't all that normal in local government. It was less prevalent as a style than it currently is, I think.

*I have some vague memory that Newcastle was the first to have a chief executive, wasn't it? Before that, it was just a town clerk …*
Yes, it was a town clerk. There were changes of that kind, yes.

*So you came on Newcastle Council in the years of opposition. What was it like then, being a new councillor and being in opposition?*
Well, it was very exciting. I mean there was, of course, the important work in the ward. The council was quite lively. I enjoyed the debating part of the council chamber, and the ward work and the whole thing.

*Had you honed your debating skills at the RGS and Oxford?*
Yes. Chair of the debating society at school. Chair of the Labour Club at Oxford and so on. I didn't do anything in the Oxford Union though.

*Was that part of what oiled your career in the Party in Newcastle, that you were an effective debater?*
Probably, yes. I suppose it must have done, in a way.

*You're the master of the short, witty speech.*
That's kind of you to say so.

*Did you rise quickly through the Labour Group?*
Yes, I did. I became secretary in a couple of years, then chair of the group

fairly early on, and of course I was the leader before '77.

### *What were the kind of issues that you battled out in that period in opposition?*

It was basically the usual things. It was everything really. It was a bloody awful Tory council. So when we came in in the seventies we had a detailed programme, and put it through. Social services became my particular thing. That was my most productive time in politics. Later on I led a group of people, and we had this working group for months; produced a quite substantial document which went to the City Party. And, when we got in, implemented it.

### *Because of the boundary changes, did you know you were going to get in?[1]*

No. We didn't take that for granted. Of course, we were rather nervous about the changes and the fact that we had Gosforth coming in, but on the other hand we had the west end as well, that's true, but we weren't complacent at all about it. But we did win comfortably. And we were ready. At least I was ready for the social services job. And Brian Roycroft, of course, was terrific as Chief Officer. And so my four years were very productive. One year, as it were, of preparation, because the City Council took over properly in '74. The election was in '73, so there was a slightly odd period of sort of 'government in opposition'. It was a strange sort of period.

### But all you could do at that period was plan?

Exactly. Actually in some ways it was probably a blessing to do that because you had time to get stuff properly ready before you actually assumed the responsibilities.

---

1. In 1974 the Newcastle City Council boundaries expanded significantly to take in the former coalmining area to the west, which had previously been covered by Newburn Urban District Council, and the predominantly middle class area of Gosforth to the north.

*Were there some difficulties in taking in areas like Newburn that had been rock solid Labour for ever and bringing them into a small city with a sense of itself?*

Well, bit of factionalism in a way, but there always has been. But I don't think there was a problem. We looked at what was already there in terms of social services in what became the west and there was no great tension at all between the newcomers and the old city hands, as it were.

*For people who don't know the city and its politics, can you just talk generally about the 1970s, before you took power and afterwards. What was going on in the city and what did you have to do to change it?*

Well, nothing was going on: that's the reality.

*You had the Dan Smith period. And immediately afterwards there were huge plans, massive transformation of the city. I'm not thinking so much of social services as of the physical change in the city. When the Tories then came in, they didn't reverse that, did they?*

No, no.

*They vaguely and halfheartedly just carried it on?*

Yes.

*So it wasn't that they did nothing.*

Well, they didn't do anything new. And they didn't meet the needs that were so evident in other areas of policy, like education, social services ... I'd look at it the other way round: what did we do when we did get in that they hadn't done. It was enormous in social services in particular, which was my baby for four years. Transformed the bloody thing. Went from a welfare rights service to a huge increase in home help, housebuilding, the investment in schools. It was a massive change. It improved people's life-chances in the city. Also, working with the university which was just

149

beginning to mature – the council was welcoming to that and supported all of that. And we supported the Arts. There was Northern Arts, and that was supported, which had never happened before to any significant extent. And we tried to get something moving in the wider area as well, which has been off and on for decades in various forms. I was an advocate of setting up a North East Regional Councils Association, which we set up in the early eighties, I think it was. And we got that through. It wasn't the North East though, it was the North because Cumbria was in there. In fact the chair was from there – a good guy. I was the vice chair of that when we started it, and I was active in trying to promote the concept of having a more regional approach to the problems of the area. That's always been a bit difficult for people from Newcastle to do, of course, because of this historic resentment of the place that is still with us. But we did actually get stuff moving on that, which is important. And, you know, just generally did what good modern councils should do in terms of looking at their communities, seeing what the needs were, trying to meet them. And on the whole for a good few years we managed to do that. But then, of course, when there was a Tory government, it got increasingly difficult.

*In the meantime, you had this concern already for areas like Benwell. And then you'll have noticed, as the seventies went on, the dramatic disappearance of basically the industrial infrastructure. Where did that fit into your thinking?*
Well, the Priority Areas Project was my baby.[2] It was setting up the ward teams with what was actually by current standards a substantial round of funding. That was my idea. It's not really as good as it should be now because it's under-resourced, and there's no chance of restoring it. It's not nothing, but it's not what I intended it to be.

2. The Priority Areas Project was an innovative programme set up in Newcastle during the 1970s as part of an effort to tackle inequalities between areas of the city. The most deprived wards were given a budget and allocated a dedicated officer to organise regular meetings between the elected council members and representatives of different departments with local organisations and residents.

*Did you have any awareness then of just how fundamental the changes in industry and employment in the area were? People barely talked about multinationals. We didn't use words like globalisation and deindustrialization.*

The Armstrong thing was the critical event, wasn't it? The closure of the Armstrong works was really a massive blow, but also a huge message about the changes that were going on, which is why we were trying to promote the idea of regional developments. But we weren't getting very far.

*So that seemed something that local government could barely touch?*

We could influence in a way, but we didn't have the financial resources to contribute to the sort of investment that was needed. And of course there was also the problem of competition between the areas in the region, which needed to be resolved. Which is why we needed a proper regional structure, which I advocated. I knew if I put something out under my name it would never get anywhere, so I gave it to the Leader of Northumberland and he distributed it without attribution, and then we set up the regional association.

*But nationally, there was basically a big debate going on in the Labour Party about the future of government's relationship to industry – Tony Benn being industry minister pushing for planning agreements and all that sort of thing. What did you think about all that?*

It would have been good if you could have got it, but it just didn't materialise, did it? And of course, thinking back, compared to now, I think the issue now is that more of industry is not UK owned. You didn't have overseas owned car manufacturers in those days, for example. I think it's probably more difficult now, given the extent of overseas investment in the economy, nationally and locally.

2.(cont.) As well as distributing grants, it had the key aim of 'bending' council spending and services towards the needs of the worst-off areas rather than those in which residents were able to shout the loudest. Although its funding and anti-poverty focus were progressively diluted over time, the Priority Areas Project turned out to be one of the longest lasting projects promoting community engagement in particular localities in any local government area.

*That wasn't a debate you were particularly involved in?*
No.

*Arguably it was a key moment about whether you just open up to globalisation and let it rip, or whether you try and build structures to ...*
It didn't happen anyway.

*No, it didn't happen. Okay, but then ... I can't date this ... even before Thatcher came in, the Labour Government had actually put a stop to the expansion of local government spending – you know, the whole thing about Crosland and "the party's over". So there were cuts. And also, presumably by implication, reductions in the power of local government. How did you react to that?*
Well, it was extremely disappointing, but there was an economic crisis, which people tend to forget about. So we were in a particularly difficult epoch really.

*So basically you had this wonderful period from 1974 to about '78 when you actually could expand services and deliver according to needs, and then that was slowed down..*
It was slowed down and then it started to go into reverse.

*So was that the heyday of local government as well, in a way, that period? When you actually could do things?*
I'd say so. It's up to other people to make the judgement. My best years in local government, certainly.

*You had more power and flexibility than you were to have later?*
I think I did in some respects. I'm not sure in relation to the local economy we had greater influence. We had some influence because we owned land in the city and so on, which was important, and we were funding stuff obviously …

**But you were able to directly deliver services which, a decade later, you had to put out for competitive tendering, for example, and you had rate capping …**

That's right.  And we had a public transport system and the rest of it.

**Oh yes, you still owned the buses, didn't you?**

Absolutely.  All that went.  So much of major stuff is contracted out now.

**So looking back at that period of the seventies, what would you see as your greatest achievement?**

Social Services.  When I was Chair of Social Services.

**That was your choice, to be Chair of Social Services?**

Yes

**Why particularly?**

I was just interested in it.  It was triggered, I think, basically by just seeing how people were living in Benwell and the West End really – and the needs there that were not being met.  And we provided a way of tackling these problems.  And we did.  It was a very productive time for a few years.

**I don't know how to put it really, but how would you see your role in local government – your commitment to public service. In your own words, how would you describe it?**

It's about trying to promote a better society, a more equal society, at a local level, as part of what ought to be a national approach to the issue.  It's promoting equality, as far as you can do it, and that includes things like endeavouring to support the local economy as well as directly providing services.  That's got to be the core of what local government is about.

**What about being a local councillor, and being elected for a particular area, what does that mean to you?**

It's important to have a constituency, as it were, where you are dealing with a range of issues that affect people. You've got to know as far as you can – and of course it's not easy – what are the issues that demand attention. And that means looking to, obviously, your constituents, but also the organisations in the patch, and trying to listen to them. And trying to reflect that in the council's policy, but also trying to influence the government of the day. So it's not a single path you're going down but several paths that you have to proceed down to get things to move. And you've got to convince people that you have to invest in people and in the services that they require.

*You always seem to me to be remarkably constant in your political principles and so on over the years, which makes you unusual in the Labour Party. We used to joke about the fact that I used to see you on the right, and then the whole Labour Party seemed to move, leaving you looking like a raving leftie. Do you represent a strand in the Labour Party of commitment to public services and local government that has pretty much died out?*

No, I don't think it has died out but it's not sufficiently recognised in the Party. No, it hasn't died out. I don't think that's fair to say.

### What about the Parliamentary Labour Party though?

Well, God knows where they are. I've been attending the PLP now for ten years, and there's a good deal of support for local government there. It hasn't always translated adequately into government, it's fair to say, although compared with what we've got now it was nirvana, even in the hard years of the Labour Government. And there was always something you could get out of the previous Labour administration, if not enough. But nothing like as disastrous as the present situation. I mean here we are now £330m short of where we were in 2010. It's unbelievable.

*Can I ask: if you'd been in government in the nineties etc, would you have gone along the route of all those initiatives, setting up quasi-*

154

*democratic structures like Single Regeneration Budget, New Deal for Communities, Sure Start or would you have mainly pumped the money into local government and the NHS in areas?*

I'd have gone for both really. They are both contributors to the transformation we need. I don't think it's one or the other. You have to have a mix of both. Because there's some stuff that has to be nationally funded, and more or less nationally delivered, but it has to be seen as part of a coherent policy across local and national services. And there needs to be a relationship between, for example, the NHS and local government.

*So again, looking back at that period of the seventies what, if any, regrets do you have about what you might have done differently, or things that didn't work out, or …*

I don't think I have much in the way of regrets in the seventies. I think we did a very good job in the seventies in the city. It got more difficult after that, particularly with the Tory Government. But now! It was bad enough in the eighties, but it's infinitely worse now than it's ever been. A good way of testing that is to see how Tory councils are reacting to all the Tory government is doing. It's unprecedented. They're howling as much as we are – well, some of them anyway. And we are 25 years on from having a Tory councillor in the city.

The other thing I just want to touch on is community relations, because I was always keen on that and supportive of working with the BME communities, and I think I can claim to have perhaps influenced that in a constructive way, as opposed to either doing nothing or being difficult about it, as it were, from their perspective.

*So did you put money into the likes of the Community Relations Council?*

Not much in the way of money, but there was a lot of access and support and discussion. They always said that they had the best relationships, as far as I could see, between the communities and the council of anywhere. The other thing, of course, we had a committee system in those days.

*That was New Labour, wasn't it, elected mayors ...[3]*

It's striking. The council meetings now are just theatrical. They're not really approving anything. The committee system is appalling. No proper reports. And that means people are more detached. Not everyone would participate fully, but there are enough people who would, in a committee system, not just facilitate scrutiny but also to get some thinking done and some policymaking. And that is gone really. I regret that very much.

## A CAREER IN LOCAL GOVERNMENT: A FOOTNOTE

**The following edited extracts are taken from an earlier interview with Jeremy recorded by Judith Green in a Newcastle restaurant. It took place on 2 May 1995, two years before New Labour took power and during Blair's efforts to reform the Party, including the scrapping of Clause Four. The interview mainly focused on the details of policy and services in Newcastle, but, as these extracts show, there are some interesting insights into Jeremy's political perspectives and career choices.**

*Do you see this as a historic moment for the Labour Party?*

Yes, it's the equivalent of what the German SPD did when they formally abandoned Marxism. I think it's a sign of maturity that we recognise that you can't parrot slogans indefinitely as a substitute for actual thinking. We ought to be thinking more about how we regulate a mixed economy and how we protect consumers including consumers of public services, and we become less of an old fashioned producerist party as the economy becomes less of an old fashioned producing economy in the sense that it used to be.

---

3. One of the the Labour Government's reforms was to restructure local government, forcing them to move away from the previous system of committees. Councils had to choose between an elected mayor and a cabinet system. Jeremy was a strong opponent of elected mayors.

*I didn't understand why it was necessary to pitch the battle at that symbolic level at that time.*

I thought that at first. But I think he was right. I think the Party has got to be made to face up to bloody reality. It's no good coasting along on nostalgia – memories of 1945 and all that – and expecting that history is running our way. It just isn't. In practice we have for a long time accepted the mixed economy. Now we have to own up to that reality, and sort out the level of public intervention that's necessary in terms of ownership or regulation or just participation. Because after all, ownership has changed since 1918 so radically, hasn't it? Management and control is still in the hands of a small number of people, but they don't own the businesses any more. Ownership is much more diffuse and much more widespread than ever it was, through pension funds, insurance portfolios and the like. We need to change how some of these decisions are made. Not the same as Lord Londonderry owning the mines any more. It is different. And Clause Four couldn't allow for that, and we weren't facing up to the real issues partly because of it. We were just like MacDonald in the twenties. We can't actually do anything because the grand utopia is so far ahead, so we'll just kind of bump along. That's really been our position for 30 years. If you're waiting for some kind of transforming economic revolution, you just sit down like a millenarian and wait for the Messiah to appear. It's hopeless.

**What is your future?**

That depends on the leadership of the Party. If he puts me in the Lords, I'll go there. Otherwise I'll stay here and do things locally and nationally.

**Do you regret not becoming an MP?[4]**

Not at all. I'd have gone spare. Can you imagine if I'd got in in 1974?

4. Jeremy stood for election as MP for Tynemouth at an early stage in his career, and later attempted unsuccessfully to gain the nomination for a Newcastle seat. His options were limited by his commitment to Tyneside, and he did not engage in the usual route for aspiring Labour candidates of hawking themselves around the country.

### You'd have been Leader!

Actually it's funny you should say that. It did spasmodically occur to me. On the other hand, I wouldn't have been here, and I'd have missed so much of the kids – and for what? For 20 years in opposition and the off-chance of being a cabinet minister for a few years. No regrets at all.

### Were you ever tempted to take the Liverpool route?[5] Would history have been different?

Yes. We would have been out of power in Newcastle. You don't see me as the Lenin of Tyneside, do you? Leading an authoritarian charge? What are you supposed to do, for God's sake? Go rampaging through the streets of Gosforth, smashing Mercedes or something?

---

5. A reference to the position taken by some local authorities in opposition to the Thatcher Government.

*Life is short:*
*the fruit of this life*
*is a good character*
*and acts for the common good.*

'Meditations'
Marcus Aurelius
121-180 AD